West End: renewal of a metropolitan centre

West End: renewal of a metropolitan centre

by Kenneth Browne

The Architectural Press, London

First published 1971
© Kenneth Browne 1971
ISBN 0 85139 664 X

Printed in Great Britain by Robert MacLehose & Co Ltd
The University Press, Glasgow

Contents

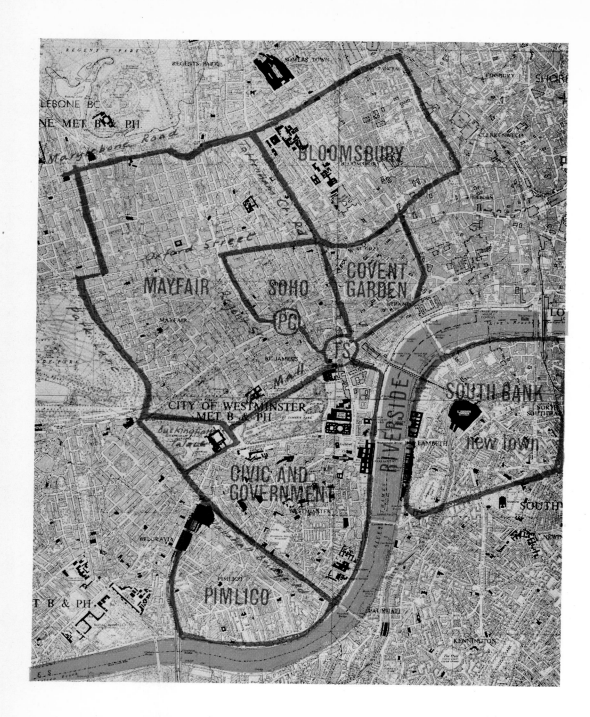

Introduction

This book, which is based on a series of articles reprinted from the *Architectural Review*,* attempts to look at London's West End in a special kind of way; to study its qualities and problems as urban landscape. Its object is to encourage both a more sympathetic understanding of what exists and at the same time a more imaginative approach to conservation and renewal.

Today we are threatened on all sides by fragmentation of our environment – the pieces no longer add up, everything becomes more and more unrelated. If we are to reverse this drift to chaos, it is essential that we try to understand how continuity of environment can

* Mainly in 1966/67 with the exception of Covent Garden which appeared in 1964.

be achieved. We must concern ourselves not just with special buildings but with our *surroundings*, particularly the spaces between buildings and our total experience of the townscape.* One of the main points stressed by the authors of *Traffic in Towns** was that, in built-up areas, major roads must run between areas of homogeneous character, never through them. Where this proved impossible, then they must run above or below pedestrian level so that continuity would not be broken. The result would then be a road network serving, not disrupting, the environment.

It follows then that it is fundamentally important to define the boundaries of such areas as soon as possible; and also to treat individual trouble spots such as (in the case of the West End) Piccadilly Circus, Trafalgar Square, Parliament Square, etc., not as isolated problems, the present way, but as aspects of one big problem. On the map opposite, the West End is shown roughly parcelled off into areas of distinctive character, and in the following chapters they are examined as urban landscape and an attempt made to find the significant connections between them.

The traffic surveys now in progress will determine the desire-lines of vehicles, but it is essential and most urgent that they should be parallelled by townscape surveys. These should be in considerable detail and define all the environmental qualities which are worth keeping. Also the inherent possibilities in human and spatial terms. This means no less than mapping and recording all good groups of buildings, good spaces, good views; adding up to an appreciation of present environment and potential to set against the requirements of traffic.

It boils down to making clear what is important about each place, for if this is not comprehended before replanning starts, then character is bound to go; there can be no continuity and everything will tend to become anonymous mush.

Today, with some justification, emphasis is on easing traffic, but in human terms – in terms of town rather than ant heap – the opposite approach of safeguarding good environment is essential. The way things are going no good environment will be left by the time we wake up to the importance of protecting it. The City of London is a dreadful warning in this respect. There the abysmal failure to grasp the great opportunities provided by the blitz, the haphazard scattering of huge office blocks, and the destruction of some of the best environment for traffic routes,* show the vital need for a more imaginative attitude to urban values elsewhere in the capital. As it is, planning is all too often destructive of environment. Without a proper survey of what exists planning is blind and architecture unrelated.

In limited space it is only possible to outline the sort of townscape surveys which are needed if irreplaceable things are not to be swept away, by accident as much as bloody-mindedness. The object is to make people look again at places whose image has been dulled by familiarity and see how they could be improved and related; for townscape is particularly this art of seeing the connections.

In practice, each area needs a painstaking check-list defining: (1) present character; (2) what is good (buildings, shapes, etc.); (3) what bad; (4) important viewpoints; (5) pointers (levels, etc.); (6) where traffic is acceptable and at what density; (7) suggestions arising from all this.

* The importance of caring for more than the isolated special buildings has at last been recognised in the Civic Amenities Act of 1967, which requires local authorities to designate *areas* of special architectural or historic interest which should be preserved.

* *Traffic in Towns. A study of the long-term problems of traffic in urban areas.* HMSO, 1963.

* For instance the splendid line of riverside warehouses off Upper Thames Street, the one example in London of Venice-like immediacy between buildings and river, a favourite subject for painters.

*St Martin-in-the-Fields framed by
the portico of the National Gallery*

Trafalgar Square

In his traffic report for the Whitehall study* Professor Buchanan suggested workable routes for a primary road network for London. These presented some fearful problems of environment, particularly in the Trafalgar Square area (TS on map) where two primaries would cross. 'In fact,' he said, 'the Trafalgar Square area presents so many problems that it requires a special study of its own.'

It seems logical then to take Trafalgar Square, London's main pedestrian concourse, its centre and one of its four busiest traffic intersections – a place where, as Buchanan says, 'the conflict between traffic and environment is acute' – as the first of these townscape studies to show the kind of analysis needed, albeit in greater detail.

* *Whitehall. A Plan for the National and Government Centre.* HMSO, 1965.

Townscape Analysis

London's great civic space, its forum; the base of Nelson's column a ready-made platform for public oratory. Though once described by Sir Robert Peel as 'the finest site in Europe', it is sadly disappointing by comparison with the other great spaces in Europe. The steep fall from north to south seems to throw the whole thing off balance and except on the north side, massive chunks of building stand around as unrelated to each other and the square as a lot of bulky sideboards pushed out of place for the decorators. Immensely popular with the tourists however. But the fact that the square could be greatly improved must be recognised when plans are laid to untangle the traffic. Care must be taken not to jettison the good things with the bad.

Good Things

Interest: plenty to look at; constant movement of swooping pigeons, fountain jets and swirling red buses. Also purposeful statues well raised up against the sky, especially the finely silhouetted equestrian George IV (Chantrey) and exquisite Charles I (le Sueur).

Change of level from road and terrace to square well handled on north side with strong flights of steps angling round the statue plinths and lines of giant bollards (Barry).

Scale: suitably large, giving the right sense of a special public space and culminating in the soaring vertical of Nelson's column, its enormous base guarded by Landseer's huge but friendly lions. The column also serves to pin down the square. Space defined by lines of monumental bollards.

Variety of Surroundings: church, theatre, art gallery, shops (though not accessible enough), shipping line offices, views to Parliament.

Buildings: only the north side of the square is well defined; by the long facade of the National Gallery and centred by its portico and dome. The steeple and side-on view of the portico of St. Martin-in-the-Fields (Gibbs) splendidly hold the north-east corner. Facing the north side of the church (and therefore out of sight from the square) the fine clean cut stucco facade of St. Martin's National School (Taylor) must be kept. Otherwise only Canada House (former Royal College of Physicians – by Smirke) on the west of the square has any merit.

Bad Things

Square now isolated by a sea of traffic (see picture below), giving no feeling from the outside of being usable public space. The great scrimmage of traffic at the top of Whitehall (Charing Cross) particularly daunting. The 'full tide of life' admired here by Dr. Johnson having now become a lethal tide of metal.

Nelson's column is uncomfortably placed on the very edge of the traffic stream.

Inclined roads to east and west sides distort perspective.

Square loses shape at south end where space slides away.

This is a huge, draughty space with an inadequate feeling of enclosure. No shelter from weather except down the subways, therefore often bleak and inhospitable.

Nowhere to get even a sandwich without braving the traffic. Completely isolated from shops, restaurants, pubs.

Lacks trees – those on north side have been felled and reveal the whole of the National Gallery which seen this way is a rather uninspired building.

Surrounding buildings generally poor save for north side. Their irregular skyline, lack of relationship, and indifferent design make an unsatisfactory wall to the square. South Africa House particularly clumsy.

1 **2** **3**

Viewpoints

1. Very good approach down St. Martin's Lane stopped by the spire of St. Martin-in-the-Fields, the projecting portico hinting at the unseen space that faces it.

2. Closer view on same approach – note the way the entrance to Trafalgar Square is pinched between the church portico and the National Gallery (they are not parallel on plan). Trafalgar Square itself announced by the sudden exclamation mark of Nelson's column, rising from spray of fountains.

3. Several framed views from the National Gallery portico which is a very special vantage point, particularly the splendid view down Whitehall to the spires of Westminster – the ceremonial way – where the tower of Big Ben answers Nelson's column. Note curve of Whitehall which is very important as it ensures that the fine backcloth of towers changes as you go down the street – any suggestion of blocking this Whitehall vista or straightening it should be resisted.

4 **5** **6**

4. Also the fine visual link between the Gallery and St. Martin's church – another portico at right angles (see page 8).

5. Exit from Grand Arcade giving framed view of National Gallery. Not so much to keep, but as a pointer to the sort of thing needed in any new scheme.

6. The exciting concentration of verticals; Nelson's column, St. Martin's spire, Coliseum tower, statues, fountains – especially concentrated from the Admiralty Arch. Also (not illustrated), the view in from Pall Mall with three porticos, starting with that of Canada House on the right.

Pointer: steep groundfall across the square from north to south, continuing for some way down Whitehall.

Recommendations

— Sink traffic in front of National Gallery* so that it and St. Martin's church appear to be on a podium above the traffic, with bridges over it and monumental steps down to the square, 7. From the National Gallery link north via pedestrian alleyways of small shops to Leicester Square, 8. The level of the latter might be raised above that of the traffic to facilitate connection with the suggested two-level Piccadilly Circus to the west. To the east a pedestrian route could be carried over the traffic of Charing Cross Road to connect with Covent Garden.

— Make use of the steep fall in levels down to Whitehall. Sink level on south side of square (Charing Cross) to general level of Whitehall and continue existing floor of the square over it, bringing Nelson's column more comfortably into the square itself. Provide steps and ramps down to Whitehall.

— Re-route traffic to remove it from east and west sides of square and form an upper promenade on both sides with small shops, kiosks, cafes and pubs underneath (also entrance to Underground). These would help to humanize the space. Large shops would face onto the promenade itself overlooking the square.

— Plant more trees. Rebuild the sides of the square, save for north side and perhaps Canada House, and provide arcade links, on the lines of the existing Grand Arcade, opening out to sudden dramatic views of the square, 9.

* As suggested by W. K. Smigielski in his second-prize-winning scheme in the New Roads for London 1960 competition.

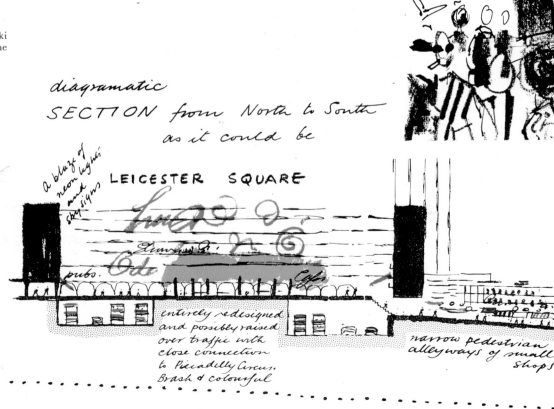

diagramatic
SECTION from North to South
as it could be

a blaze of neon lights and sky signs

LEICESTER SQUARE

pubs.

entirely redesigned and possibly raised over traffic with close connection to Piccadilly Circus. Brash & colourful

narrow pedestrian alleyways of small shops

National Gallery

upper square

St Martin in the Fields

Hotel Bruges

arcades

7

St Martins

National Gallery

TRAFALGAR SQUARE

bridges over traffic

vantage point

road in cutting

the great open air forum dignified by large scale – statues, fountains and vista

ground falls N to S · · · 3

The National Gallery is really too low to contain the top of the square. Suggest that this might be helped by controlled high building in regular line behind it on the south edge of Leicester Square, but this would need very careful handling.

Link to Covent Garden area through a series of pedestrian squares and passageways, starting off with a pedestrian square between St. Martin's and the National Portrait Gallery. The present space is cut up by the traffic and needs humanizing by the introduction of shops on the north side, 11.

Arcades would lead into the square at promenade level, connected to other pedestrian spaces.

9

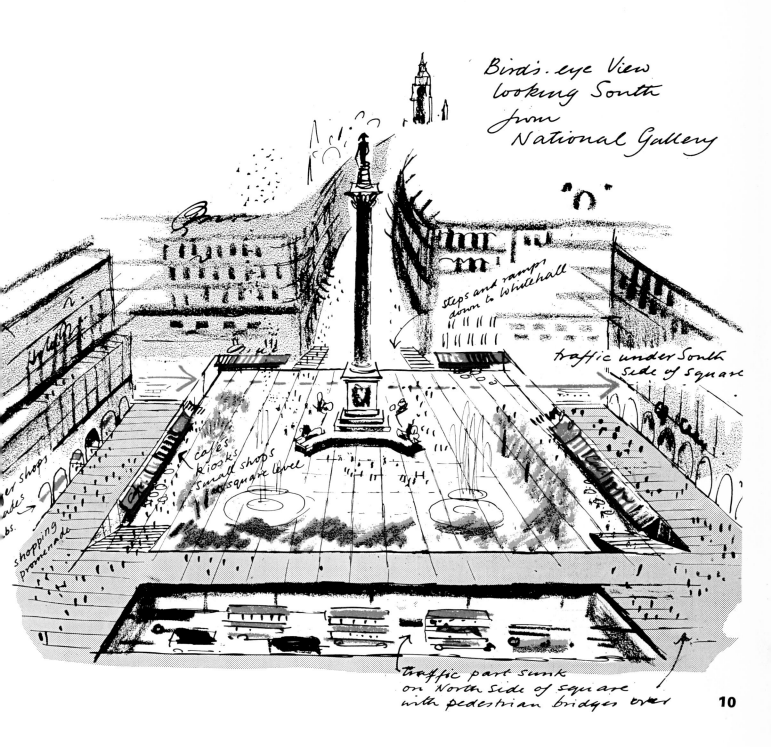

Birds-eye View
looking South
from
National Gallery

steps and ramps
down to Whitehall

traffic under South
side of square

cafes
kiosks
small shops
at square level

shopping
promenade

er shops
ades
bs.

'O'

traffic part sunk
on North side of square
with pedestrian bridges over

10

St Martins in the Fields

Trafalgar Square

The National Gallery

Kenneth Browne

11

Soho

The dreary tendency for everywhere to become more and more the same, for character to be ironed out, and for every problem to ring up the same standard solution, is surely a sad reflection on modern town planning. Must we accept this process as inevitable; a mad corruption of the idea of equal opportunities for all? If not, then somehow town planning must become the vital, life-giving force it has so far failed to be. It must lead, not drift with the developer. This makes it essential that the planners recognize and value the differences between places, emphasizing not destroying them.

For example, nowhere in London is more different, more itself, than Soho, the tight-packed, raffish jungle north of Piccadilly Circus. Yet its particular character depends almost entirely on that mixture of uses so disliked by tidy minds. Architecture as such means little, but the general height of the buildings (four or five storeys on average) and the small size of the shops which give the scale matters very much. Only in the case of the two squares and the buildings facing the ends of the narrow streets (75 Beak Street is a good example) do you have room to stand back and look at the elevations. Generally, all is so tightly compacted that it is the signs, sunblinds, lettering and people that count – all the things near eye level.

The special character of Soho is defended by making entrance seem more difficult (see facing page). For instance, by the chasm of Sutton Row, far right, the blockade of Great Windmill Street, top right, or the shell hole of Air Street, bottom. Inside, spatial pressure is maintained by such townscape effects as that in Berwick Street market, top left.

Boundaries

Bounded by intensely busy traffic routes (see map, below) Soho is shaped like an axe head, the shaft being Charing Cross Road and the cutting edge Regent Street. The top edge is Oxford Street and the bottom, less clear, is strictly Shaftesbury Avenue but in fact Soho merges here with Theatreland down to the line of Coventry Street and Leicester Square. The strongest boundary is the splendid Nash sweep of Regent Street which effectively seals off Soho from fashionable Mayfair to the west. The very activity

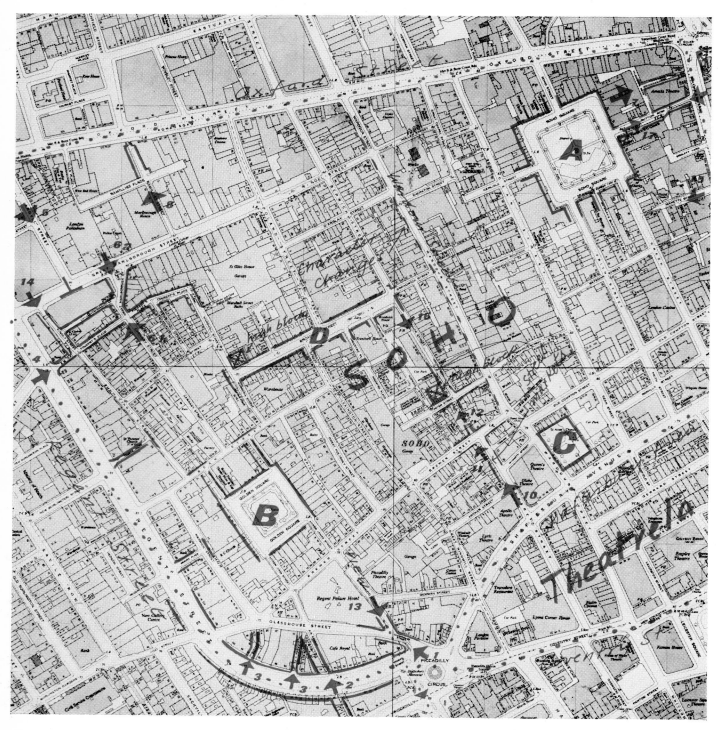

of the perimeter roads which reaches fever pitch at the corner intersections of Piccadilly, Cambridge, St. Giles and Oxford Circuses, serves to isolate the centre block.

Character

The exotic character of Soho is too well known to need much amplification. Land of good eating and striptease, it is a human pin-table, with serial vision of a special kind. Continental London, the kasbah, its cafes, espresso bars, street markets, and endless permutations of alleys, byways and elusive streets add up to a fascinating inner city. In addition it has perhaps more early eighteenth-century houses which are actually lived in than almost any part of London. East of Wardour Street the pattern is a fairly orderly criss-cross of streets but west of it the maze really winds up.

This intricacy is particularly noticeable by contrast with the scale of the busy streets on the perimeter and most strikingly with the enormously civilized sweep of Regent Street. There are strong contrasts inside Soho too, like the narrow pedestrian Meard Street where eighteenth-century houses, still used as such, face non-stop striptease clubs.

How does Soho keep its character? First of all by being a maze. Streets are narrow and few run straight through, so traffic is slow and a leisurely street life becomes possible with street corner conversation and street markets. How is it contained? The answer seems to be by making things difficult. First, by the moat of traffic on all four sides. Second, by making penetration of the perimeter wall seem to be hard.

Entrances and Exits

Some of the ways in which this happens are traced in sketches 1 to 12.

Wedge: for instance, starting at Piccadilly Circus, if you look north up Glasshouse Street the entrance to Soho is visually blocked by the wedge of the Regent Palace Hotel acting like a visual bung. You are made to squeeze in up Sherwood Street, 1. The feeling of restriction is later reinforced by a pedestrian bridge over the street.

Then, walking up Regent Street, there is another instance at Air Street, where the outer wall is suddenly and dramatically breached.

Shell Hole: here, rusticated arches, in series, pierce through at an angle, repeating in each layer of building, and somehow expressing the resistance. This may sound a bit fanciful but it is the stuff from which town character is made, 2.

Tunnel: further up Regent Street, the entrance to Soho is by two successive arcades, Quadrant and Brown's, 3.

Narrows: higher still, Foubert's Place is typical of restricted pedestrian entry, a narrow vista of shops and cafes setting the character at a glance, 4. In fact the whole of this corner (see map) is expressive and worth keeping.

End Stop: for instance coming in from Oxford Street the blocking of Argyll Street by Liberty's, 5, is followed by a subtle bit of double take, working both ways, 6, as you enter Carnaby Street from Great Marlborough Street.

Slice: the road first slides behind the 'jacobethan' mass of Liberty's then angles sharply back so that the view down Carnaby Street is blocked, 6a. Looking back from the latter, 6b, the street is stopped, not by Liberty's as you expect, but by a small Watney pub, 'The Grapes', which was hidden from Great Marlborough Street; surprise.

Arch: this most clearly expresses the idea of the gateway. It occurs at Air Street, already mentioned, and also for instance beside Liberty's, Manette Street, and Falconberg

1 Wedge   2 Shell hole   3 Tunnel   4 Narrows

5 End stop   a   b   6 Slice

"OUTSIDE"

INSIDE

7 Arch

8 Chasm

outside world

Oxford street

Court, 7 (here most dramatically combined, on looking back, with the 34-storey office tower at St. Giles' Circus).

Chasm: this dramatic entrance occurs repeatedly and a good example is shown in 8. Note that in this case, at Ramillies Street, both buildings are new and though nothing special as architecture the townscape effect is good, looking both in and out.

Side Spread: this is a development of the chasm and occurs notably at Sutton Row leading from Charing Cross Road to Soho Square, 9. The entrance is again a narrow slit, but soon the left-hand wall angles back, before continuing parallel with the opposite wall. This means that at first you see only the slit and, at the far end, the trees of Soho Square, (a), but when the street doubles in width the tower of St. Patrick's church on the far corner comes suddenly into the picture, (b). Extra width also gives the chance to stand far enough away to see it properly. The view back is again a winner, the fretted surface of the giant tower block zooming up through the entrance slit (see page 19).

Decoy: this is an important townscape gambit to effect transition from one district to another. The sequence up Rupert Street (10 to 12), shows the decoy at work and is also a prime example of multiple use. The foreground street market leading in from Shaftesbury Avenue is an immediate magnet, busy, noisy, colourful. Yet straight ahead the way looks blocked. This is typical: the secret world defended, 10. However the neon sign of a revue bar at the far end beckons irresistibly. Then, turning left at the end, a narrow footpath, Walker's Court, pierces the wall of Brewer Street, 11. Narrow and claustrophobic, lined with 'caffs' and nude book shops, the space is further compressed by a footbridge overhead. Suddenly the eye is carried upwards as a tall block of flats comes into view, 12. Out then into Berwick Street and one of the busiest open-air markets in London. Market stalls jam up the roadway, parallelled by an arcade of shops down the west side. And looking back from higher up Berwick Street, you get one of the best views in Soho; these are just a few of the ways in which the street world is contained. In many cases the buildings concerned are nothing architecturally speaking, yet the lessons they give in terms of space control are important.

SOHO SQUARE

← Soho Square

a

Side spread

b

9

CHARING CROSS RD.

Strippers

Non Stop

Spectacular

Ripe

10

The Interior

The feeling of the kasbah is maintained inside the walls by such townscape devices as the dogleg, the T-junction, and the wing, the street lengths being kept short and thus maintaining the sense of a place to loiter rather than to rush through. Also the buildings are fairly low, and it is important that the existing average height should be kept as it contributes to human scale.

Interlock: in the area west of Wardour Street the street pattern sometimes has the intricacy of an interlocking puzzle. Elsewhere however, the centre seems to have gone dead and you feel that the voltage is highest within striking distance of the perimeter; for instance Carnaby Street.

Rests: the maze would become unbearable without stopping places to rest feet and take bearings and it is here that the squares come in, with the few high buildings as reference beacons. In this category there are two real squares (both dating from the time of Charles II and once fashionable and domestic in character), a churchyard and an oblong length of street.

Soho Square, A on plan: this is a square really squared with the corners held, not broken through by roads. Laid out in 1681 on the site of the Monmouth House, the square still has some good buildings around it which should be kept, particularly on the north side. Also, and most important, No. 1 Greek Street in the southeast corner which is a fine example of a mid-eighteenth-century town house. Any further high buildings around the square should be discouraged (see Golden Square). Splendid trees and well kept grass make this a haven from the traffic of Oxford Street but the effect is cheapened by a ludicrous Snow White summer house, which should go. The statue of Charles II (part of a larger monument by Cibber), needs elevation, and the floorscape of the square needs to be simplified. It is now far too fussy, clumsily terraced and cluttered with benches. The Italianate tower of St. Patrick's RC church on the corner is well placed.

Golden Square, B this has about four decent eighteenth-century houses around it, otherwise nothing much that is worth keeping. Once symmetrical, it is now a jumble; ruined by the violent irregularity of the skyline and the collision of scales. The central garden is pathetic; a cautionary example of what a city square should not be like. Can you imagine this in Montmartre? Pseudo-Cotswold walling, wallflowers in rows and a rather sad George II (also placed too low) standing lost in the middle of it all. A new and simpler treatment is essential with plenty of big plane trees and a better wall of buildings around the square.

St. Anne's Churchyard, C: this is dominated by Cockerell's malevolent but striking church tower, which is fortunately to be kept in the rebuilding of the ruined church. The treatment of the garden fronting on Wardour Street is important. A pleasant space and pleasantly raised up from the road level, its retaining wall is ugly and the outlook depressing, being limited to the dreary flank wall of the Queen's Theatre. This needs sympathetic treatment and perhaps partial screening from the road.

Broadwick Street: a special case; a wide stretch of road in the middle of Soho blocked both ends to form an oblong, D. The buildings generally are not up to much but the space is good and the one high block at the west end effectively holds down the space.

Viewpoint 13

Viewpoints

These need further study but there are few special viewpoints. Apart from those associated with 'Entrances and Exits', there is one of particular value. This is looking south from Sherwood Street across Piccadilly Circus, and down Lower Regent Street to the Duke of York's column and the towers of Parliament; the whole framed in the arches of the County Fire Office building, 13. This view should be kept and considered in any planning solutions to Piccadilly Circus.

Planning Guides

1. Keep the small scale, tightness and irregularity; do not try to straighten it out.

2. Encourage the existing multiple use and small shops with no zoning and no 'multiples': to quote Ian Nairn, 'This is the free port every city must have.'

3. Keep entry difficult – do not drive roads through it and break it up.

4. Discourage traffic from entering but provide, if possible, underground car parks beneath Soho – this would give the surprise of emerging into a different world from the motor scale outside.

5. High blocks. Generally keep them out – on perimeter only (because of the traffic they generate as well as the scale). However, the odd tower in the kasbah, and it must be for living and not just office accommodation, is effective as a landmark, as those at Berwick Street and the corner of Broadwick Street show. No opening out of streets to compensate; buildings must rise from the general street line. Visually they might be good at the corners of Soho, as the St. Giles' Circus tower demonstrates.

6. Keep pedestrians mainly at ground level (a section through the perimeter wall, in this case at Regent Street, might be as shown below).

7. Plot where the centre of Soho has become derelict and work out a scheme to bring it to life. This will involve rethinking some of the street shapes and perhaps creating a new square.

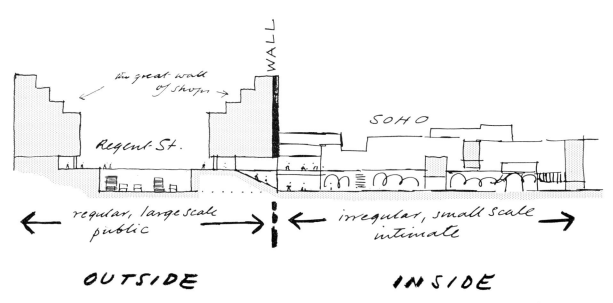

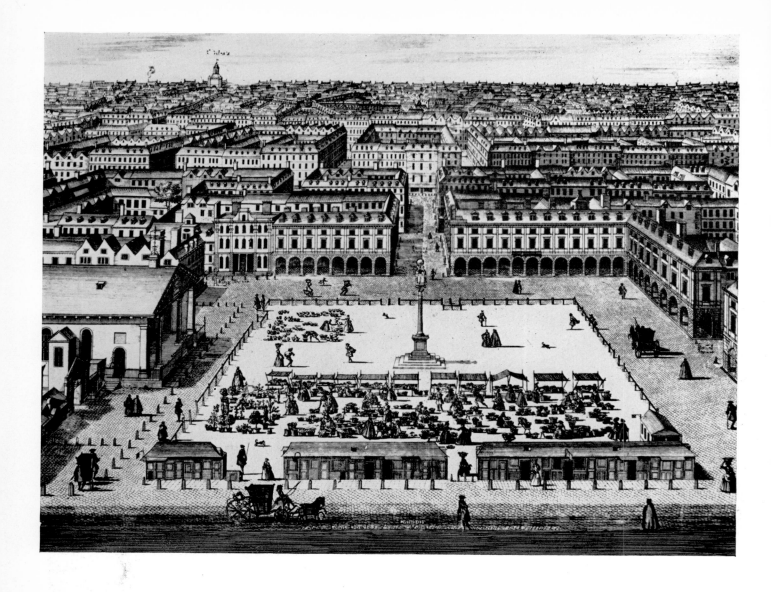

Covent Garden

For years the world famous Covent Garden Market has been crippled by acute traffic congestion and the market is now scheduled to move to Nine Elms, south of the Thames by 1972. But what of Covent Garden itself? Unless positive and creative planning measures are taken now, its special character will quickly be erased by wholesale redevelopment. * Yet it should be London's Latin quarter.

It is hard to picture Covent Garden, the urban cornucopia, without its market; without the splendid chaos which now exists; a cheek by jowl juxtaposition of bananas and ballerinas, top notes and turnips, ripe fruit and riper language. All these are the epitome of the place. As to architecture, everything and everybody is so close packed, it seems to be mainly an architecture of fruit boxes; with, of course, St. Paul's church by Inigo Jones, 'the handsomest barn in England,' jutting its hat over the high stacked diesel lorries, its portico stuffed with porters swilling back cuppas from the coffee stall. Also, round the corner in Bow Street, the Royal Opera House by E. M. Barry.

But what future has Covent Garden? The prospect is not encouraging. London, 'the

* Since this was written, the Greater London Council, Westminster City Council and Camden Borough Council have formed a consortium to study the problem. Their planning team's proposals, many of which agree with the views expressed here, were published in a report *Covent Garden's Moving*, Nov., 1968.

unique city' as Rasmussen calls it, is steadily being straightened out, having its eccentricities corrected, its character impoverished, not only by piecemeal replacement but also by the well-intentioned doctrine of the clean sweep (politely called comprehensive redevelopment). It is being made to conform to a desiccated conception of what it ought to be like, with everything in compartments and no mixing by order. It is becoming just like anywhere else. What hope then for Covent Garden? Is the sort of anonymous design which any architectural student can knock out in an evening, regardless of site, good enough for this place, the brain child of Inigo Jones? It is just too easy to imagine everything swept away and only St. Paul's church left, as a sop to the sentimentalists.

But Covent Garden is not just anywhere. Quite apart from the fruit and veg. it is a very special place and deserves a less arrogant approach. In fact, the least it deserves is that anyone redesigning it should try to understand it in townscape terms. Only then should he get down to the drawing-board and reinforce in his design what he has seen.

True, at first glance (which is as much as most improvers will spare it) there does not

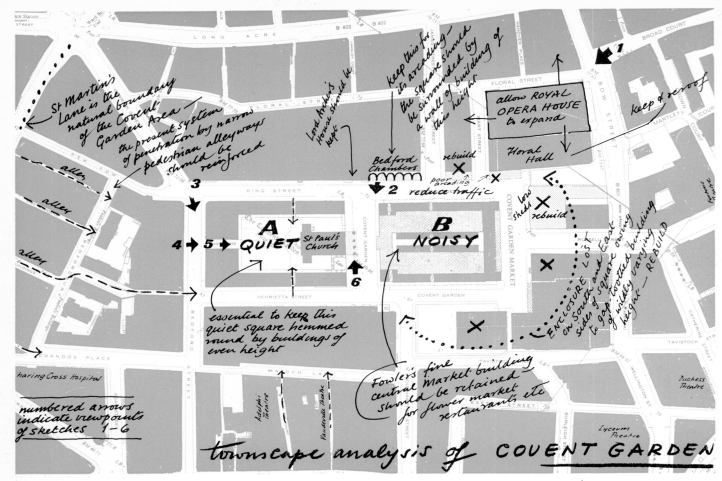

(map annotations, clockwise and around)

St Martin's Lane is the natural boundary of the Covent Garden Area

the present system of penetration by narrow pedestrian alleyways should be reinforced

keep this for its arcading — the square should be surrounded by a wall of building of this height

allow ROYAL OPERA HOUSE to expand

keep & reroof

Floral Hall

Lord Archer's House should be kept

Bedford Chambers

rebuild

poor arcading

reduce traffic

low shed — rebuild

3

2

A QUIET St Paul's Church

4 → 5 →

B NOISY

6

ENCLOSURE LOST on South and East sides of square owing to gap-toothed building of wildly varying height — REBUILD

essential to keep this quiet square hemmed round by buildings of even height

Charing Cross Hospital

numbered arrows indicate viewpoints of sketches 1-6

Adelphi Theatre

Vaudeville Theatre

Fowler's fine central Market building should be retained for flower market restaurants etc

Duchess Theatre

Lyceum Theatre

townscape analysis of COVENT GARDEN

seem to be much architecture here, but that is because the original idea has been broken. Sutton Nicholls's drawing of 1720 (page 28) shows the original layout very well: a civic square of 1630, the first square in London, bounded by arcaded buildings of equal height – the 'piazzas' – and with a Tuscan temple (St. Paul's church) axially placed, projecting into it. *

In contrast to the noisy open square there was, and still is, a quiet enclosed square (a churchyard and part of the original convent garden). Behind the church and tightly hemmed in by a wall of buildings, it is an oasis reached only through narrow tunnels and a slit passage from Bedford Street, 3, 4, 5. It is this contrast of small secret and large public squares, and the splendid rhythm of arches reinforcing the latter, that forms the essence of this essentially civilized conception; 'the first great contribution to English urbanism,' as Summerson has called it. The churchyard still exists and is a popular tree-shaded haven from the traffic. The main square exists in plan only, for the essential enclosure of buildings and the rhythm of arcading are no more. Only in the portico of St. Paul's and the arches of Bedford Chambers (a rebuild of 1880 but faithfully reproducing the civic scale of the original arcading) can you recapture the feeling of the original idea and appreciate how splendidly arches and columns frame the sky and buildings, 2, 6. The arcade not only protects the walker but presents him with an ever-changing sequence of framed views. To-day the east and south sides of the square are a gap-toothed jumble of low and high buildings which quite destroy its unity; in fact you don't even read it as a square. The middle is occupied by Fowler's fine neo-classical market buildings of 1830.

approach 3

* Rebuilt after a fire of 1795 by Thos. Hardwick.

Royal Opera House from
Broad Court 1

St.Paul's Church framed
by arcading of Bedford Chambers. 2

. surprise   4

entry

Sequence from Bedford St
to churchyard   5

The portico of St Pauls acts as skytrap and frame—

Looking Ahead

The exciting thing to realize is that Covent Garden could really be improved by new building if the original idea of a repetition of squares and arcading were followed up, not of course in eighteenth-century fancy dress, but in a modern equivalent.

As to use, the important thing is that it must be mixed. Heaven preserve us from a zoned Covent Garden whether for businessmen or culture vultures. Such a place may fit neatly on some planner's map but it has nothing to do with what is there. It is just too easy to imagine the whole site cleared to make room for an 'Inigo Jones Centre'.

No, this must be London's Latin quarter, the place where all paths cross, the kaleidoscope where everything comes together before separating out into specialized activity.

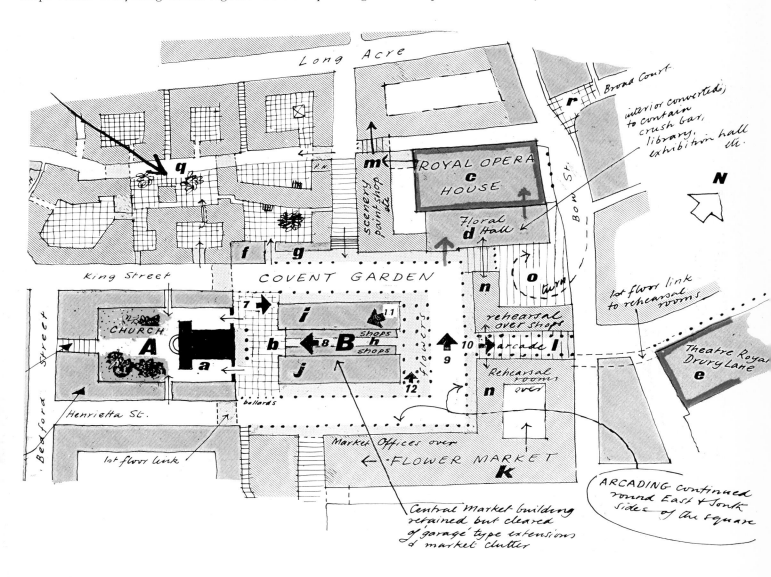

Key
a. St. Paul's Church
b. Fowl'ers Central Market
c. Royal Opera House
d. Floral Hall
e. Theatre Royal, Drury Lane
f. Lord Archer's House
g. Bedford Chambers
h. Galleria
i, j arched halls
k. flower market
l. link arcade
m. scenery block
n. rehearsal rooms
o. Approach to Floral Hall
q. Student quarter
r. Broad Court

It is a natural melting-pot for people and ideas, half-way between the City and West-minster, bordering Soho – a place where anything can happen. It should once more be a place for the cross-fertilization of opinion, where ideas buzz across the café tables like bees, as they did in the days of Johnson and Goldsmith. This give-and-take has to be reflected in the architecture; free thought cannot blossom in a gridiron. From the start, this has been a place with no closing time, where all trades and types rubbed shoulders, from the court gallants and wenches of Tom King's Coffee House to Eliza Dolittle and Professor Higgins. This atmosphere must be reinforced – a mix-up of theatres, cafés, studios, shops with their owners living over them, restaurants, students' lodgings, etc. A phony Latin quarter would make nonsense, but here it would be going with the grain; for instance:

The Royal Opera House must stay and needs room to expand. Chronically short of space for ballet and opera rehearsal, paint shops and wardrobe, it has no recording studios and at present scenery is stored either at the Docks or at Maidstone 55 km away. The Royal Ballet Schools are dispersed at Richmond and Hammersmith and the London Opera Centre is down the Commercial Road. Why not concentrate them here? The Flower Market could stay; in fact there are marketing advantages for it to do so (unlike the bulkier fruit and vegetables which should be near railways and docks). Traders want to stay. There is also a great shortage of student accommodation* and the area is well placed to provide it; in flats, hostels and studios round the square and running back from it.

* London University figures for 1961–62 showed 12,300 students in lodgings.

This line of thought is developed into a sketch scheme in the following pages. The plan on page 33 and section below, and sketches 7 to 12 show how it might look.

The main points of the scheme* are:

* Numbers refer to the sketches; letters (large and small) to the plan on page 33.

Arcading is carried right round the main square (B in plan on previous page) beneath buildings of even height, recapturing the lost sense of enclosure, 7. This enclosure is made as complete as possible by restricting vehicle entry to King Street and Henrietta Street, which could even, perhaps, be bridged over to enclose the space still further. Lord Archer's house (C 18 baroque) f, Bedford Chambers, g, and the Floral Hall, d, are retained on the north side. Otherwise there is a complete rebuild on the north, east and south sides matching Bedford Chambers for height. Any tall new buildings are towers

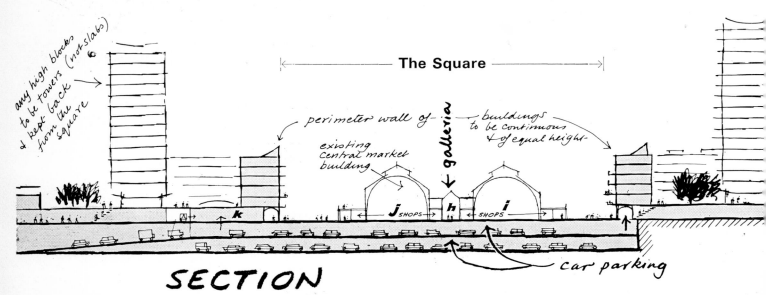

SECTION

studios

students flats

floral hall
d

any high buildings are grouped & set back from the square

rehearsal rooms

View from beside St. Paul's church looking East showing arcading carried along north and east sides of the Square.

7

not slabs, and are set back from the square (see section) so that they appear to be looking over the wall without breaking its continuity.

The Royal Opera House, *c*, is given much-needed elbow room and allowed to expand, as shown on the plan, to include the present Floral Hall, which is reroofed and redesigned inside on two levels to provide a crush bar overlooking the square, an exhibition gallery and perhaps a new and better entrance to the Opera House from the square (through the arcading as originally), 9. South of this is a rehearsal room and ballet-school block, over shops, *n*, which could be made accessible also to the Theatre Royal, Drury Lane, *e*, by a first floor link (on a colonnade) if the latter should ever join forces with the Opera House as some have suggested, 10. Expansion westward as shown would give space for scene painting, wardrobe, etc., *m*.

8

The Central Market, *b*, is retained, its perimeter colonnade answering the arcading opposite. With the present utility lean-to roofs and zoo-like cages removed, the central street, *h*, becomes a busy *galleria* of small shops, restaurants, coffee houses, and boutiques, the vista at the west end terminating in a fine close-up of St. Paul's, 8 – the columns of its portico echoed by those of the market colonnade. The shops also face outwards into the two main halls, *i, j*, glass-roofed on splendid steel arched barrel-vaults. These contain cafes, music, dancing, etc., 11. At the east end the existing forest of columns, Karnak in miniature, is a good place for the display of sample flowers, a riot of colour bursting out into the square from between the black pillars, 12. The main flower market, *k*, would be directly opposite, perhaps also occupying one of the main halls of the central market.

The Churchyard square behind St. Paul's, A p. 33, is kept, and even if the present buildings are replaced, the existing enclosure and height must be carefully repeated. No opening out here. Access to the main square is, as originally, by gateways in a high wall on either side of the church (a public lavatory now blocks one side while the other

N.E Corner of Square — as it might be — view looking towards Floral Hall with corner of square built up & arcading continuous 9

is too open visually). The squares are linked for pedestrians by two rows of bollards excluding vehicles from the space between the front of the church and the central market building.

A student quarter, *q*, of small tight-packed flats and studios, to the north-west, interspersed with pubs, small shops and cafes, is entered from the main square through the arcading under Bedford Chambers. There are also flats and studios on the upper floors around the main square itself and running back from it.

Car parking (see section). The fall of the ground, approximately 7 m., between the market and the Strand, is used to provide a reservoir of underground car-parking with direct access to the flower market and a new forecourt to the Opera House. The parking would not extend under the central market but to the south and east of it. It would also be feasible to walk through on one level from Covent Garden by bridge to the south side of the Strand and link with upper level pedestrian decks.

Arcade under rehearsal block looking towards Drury Lane —
colonnade of Theatre Royal is continued to form a visual
link (bridge over road provides physical link).

10

Galleria

The Central Market building
used for restaurants, dancing etc **11**

So much for the immediate market vicinity, but in any redevelopment, the whole Covent Garden area needs to be considered at one time and with an eye for buried treasure (see plan opposite). For instance special attention must be paid to the pedestrian links leading back from St. Martin's Lane, the natural boundary to the west, and also those up from the Strand. Also, of course, places like Broad Court, *r*, with its exciting hide-and-seek view of the Opera House, 1, and the approach to the portico of the Lyceum. Comprehensive redevelopment, that magic planning mouthful, is justified just so long as the emphasis is on comprehension (as opposed to clean sweep) and provided it denotes a willingness to see and to reinforce the good things that already exist.

Note: The author wishes to acknowledge the valuable assistance of Mr. John Kelsey in surveying the area.

Flowers displayed in the east portico
of the Central Market **12**

Plan of the
Covent Garden Area
showing some of the places
and views which must be
carefully considered in
any rebuilding

41

Theatreland

London's theatreland spreads across Soho and Covent Garden from Piccadilly Circus to the Aldwych but the lights are brightest in the triangle bounded by Charing Cross Road, Coventry Street and Shaftesbury Avenue (see map 2).

Walk east along Coventry Street and you tread the dividing line between respectability (to the south) personified by the Design Centre, the P & O and Clubland and (to the north) the gay life – the theatres and strip-clubs of Soho.

Piccadilly Circus–Leicester Square–Covent Garden; these are the key places (as opposed to streets) and in any replanning they must be considered together. Each has individual character to safeguard and the links between them need to be strengthened. At present, the connection between the first two is clear enough, but from Leicester Square to Covent Garden the route becomes confused, 3.

1

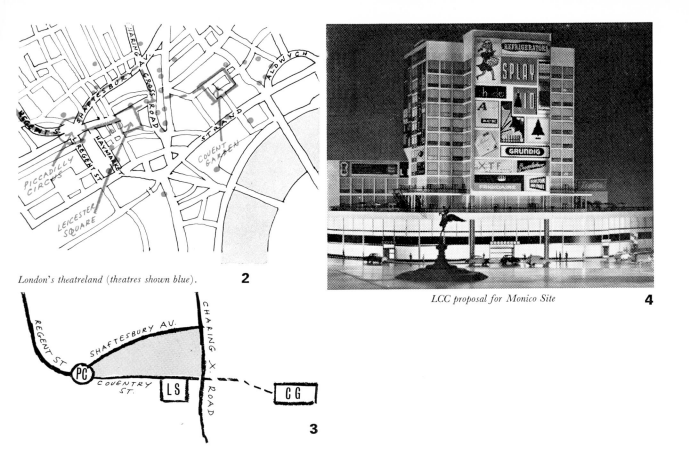

London's theatreland (theatres shown blue). **2**

LCC proposal for Monico Site **4**

3

Entry: the one really dramatic entry to theatreland occurs as you come down Regent Street. The great curve at the end restricts distant vision and it looks as though the street must go on for ever. Then suddenly everything changes. Regent Street ends abruptly with the turrets of Swan and Edgar's and architecture disappears in an explosion of erupting signs and a whirlpool of traffic. Civic architecture, in the grand manner, gives place to buildings which are no more than giant hoardings. Undignified? Perhaps, but immediately expressive of the idea of theatreland.

Piccadilly Circus

Today it is no longer a circus as Nash intended but a lopsided triangle, the result of a Board of Works decision to bisect Soho by Shaftesbury Avenue in the '80s. A large question mark has hung over it ever since Jack Cotton purchased the key Monico Restaurant site and later, in 1959, by publication of his 'Snap, Plom, For Vigor' tower,* turned Piccadilly Circus into a national issue.

* See 'Advertising into Architecture' by the author, Architectural Review, *June, 1959.*

Schemes for Rebuilding

Since then the complex problems of reconciling public and private interest, environment and traffic have bedevilled every scheme put forward; notably the Holford piazza scheme of 1961. This was based on a limitation of traffic increase to 20 per cent above the 1960 level, the most Lord Holford considered the circus would take and still leave room for pedestrians. This was subsequently scuppered by the Adams Committee's recommendation that the circus, like all major junctions in central London, must be adapted to take 50 per cent more traffic. In the absence of any overall road pattern for the future it was difficult to see how a realistic scheme for the Circus could be evolved. As Professor

43

Buchanan said, Piccadilly Circus is an intersection of streets and its future depends on what decisions are taken in respect to those streets. Such decisions cannot be taken in isolation.

However, in 1965, after further attempts at compromise, a Government working party was set up to try to end the deadlock.* It came to the conclusion that the circus must in fact be designed to take the extra traffic, and consequently came out in favour of a complete double decking of the circus with traffic at ground level and pedestrians above and below; the whole eventually linked to a double decked Regent Street. Persuaded to try yet again for a solution, despite his opposition to the idea of increased traffic, Lord Holford then produced 'Piccadilly Mark III',* described as a feasibility study only, and intended 'to form a basis for detailed engineering and architectural design'. This study accepted that as much unobstructed space as possible must be provided at street level for vehicles and proposed a raised pedestrian deck (approximately one acre in extent), not over the existing circus itself but around the perimeter, particularly on the London Pavillion site which was seen as the key to the whole problem.

* *Piccadilly Circus – Report of the Working Party.* HMSO, 1965.

* *Piccadilly Circus and the New London Pavillion.* A report by Lord Holford to the Westminster and Greater London Councils. July, 1966.

Key Site

This site became the hub of a raised circulation system, a freestanding structure supporting a deck cantilevered over the traffic. In theory any building could be placed above the deck on this site, but in the report it was visualized as a new kind of public building, perhaps a large shopping and travel centre, and to some extent an advertising hoarding.

The Circus Now

In weighing up how successful any suggested scheme might be, it is worth asking what it is that draws people to Piccadilly Circus now? For unless we are to say 'Goodbye Piccadilly' as we know it, we need to understand this. By normal design standards, it is shapeless – but in a strange way this does not seem to matter. Here Mayfair and Soho meet – the respectable and the free-and-easy – and the circus exactly expresses it.

Circus Tricks

But what are the secrets? Firstly, **Central Point** – Piccadilly Circus is the great vortex, with roads thrown off it like sparks from a Catherine wheel. Though not in fact circular, the space is pinned down by Eros at the centre of gravity – and seemingly at the centre of everything. At its spectacular best, pre-Mr. Marples and his one-way traffic system, red buses really whirled round it instead of being channelled behind railings. If Eros had in fact been put in a piazza as the 1961 scheme showed this effect of centre point would certainly have gone.

Secondly, **Wall of Lights** – apparently walled not by buildings but by giant signs which, after dark, form an architecture of light, 1, 5, nothing could better express the ephemeral world of entertainment.

Up to a point the LCC planners realized this when in their description of the new building they suggested for the Monico site they said it was to be 'designed with a comprehensive elevation treatment to receive electric advertising signs'. However, comparing it with what is there now, it's not hard to see where it would have failed. Now you get a real smack in the eye; a sign as big as a building, a bottle as big as a bus and the tracery of lights is continuous. It's vulgar but exciting. The LCC proposal was just rationed fun; controlled, co-ordinated, emasculated so that it could neither shock nor thrill. In fact it

44

reflected a guilt complex regarding posters which was quite misplaced here where the whole atmosphere depends on them. Another point: the present effect is achieved by competiton not co-ordination – the result of trying to do something more striking than the next chap – bigger and better.

With rustications of Spearmint echoing the real rustications of Swan and Edgar's, this is genuine pop art; i.e. popular with the public, a vital eruption of enthusiasm, not an imposed 'solution'. Overdesign it and the magic would vanish. The neon signs are large and close together – both important points – not separated out into polite panels as the LCC suggested, 4, which would kill the sense of free-for-all exuberance. Also the tight-packed quality prevents any one advertising slogan from dominating the whole, so the eye registers one great splash of colour. Coca-Cola is the most successful sign now, vigorously using colour, movement, and also development. The way the signs are carried round the bull-nosed corners of the buildings, is also highly effective, leading the eye out of the circus and up Shaftesbury Avenue.

Scale: these seem the biggest signs in the world because they are seen in a comparatively small space so you are bound to be close to them; the effect is most striking as you come up into the circus from the Underground. Also, they are related to Eros who is only life-size, immediately giving the measure of human scale.

Views: (a) the great view in daylight is down Lower Regent Street to Waterloo Place, a magnificent vista of the Duke of York's column and the towers of Westminster;

6

especially good when framed in the arches of the County Fire Office. (*b*) Up Shaftesbury Avenue. Eros literally flying in the sky; the curve of the theatres and the Centre Point tower in the distance.

Circus or Square?

The 1966 Holford plan in rejecting the idea of a completely decked-over circus was surely right. It is hard to see how this could ever be designed to be visually successful, especially when seen from ground level. Drawings published in the press at the time of the working party report inadvertently showed this. Anyway, a swirl of traffic is essential to the character (though how much traffic is another matter).

Less satisfactory was Holford's suggestion to turn the circus into a square, for Piccadilly Circus is really no place for squares (as the name suggests and the eye confirms). Nash designed it as a joint, not a full stop, and it would be unfortunate if his great Regent Street curve were arrested by a static shape.

Suggestions. A curve,* as shown in 7, which carried on the flow of movement would seem to be a happier solution. This could be defined by the edge of the deck and also by a great arc of illuminated signs (including a giant ticker tape), as shown in 8. In some cases freestanding sign structures could take the place of buildings for this is not the place for architecture with a capital A.

Any new buildings here must be designed for advertising – the signs not just an afterthought as they are now. But it should be taken further still. The advertising should become the architecture and be given priority in the design. Whole buildings should be used as signboards, 9, 10 – there are endless possibilities, including extending the framework of buildings to make space frames for the signs, 13. In Piccadilly Circus architecture and advertising must be indivisible.

To extend the underground concourse would undoubtedly be a good idea and the entry to it from Lower Regent Street would be made more attractive by using the levels, as 12.

* W. K. Smigielski's plan in the 'New Roads for London' competition 1959 showed Regent Street ending in a quadrant.

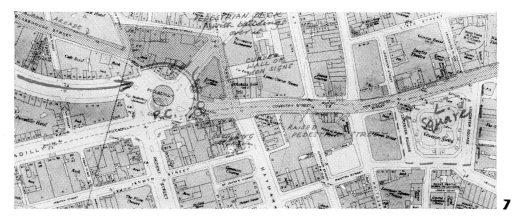

7

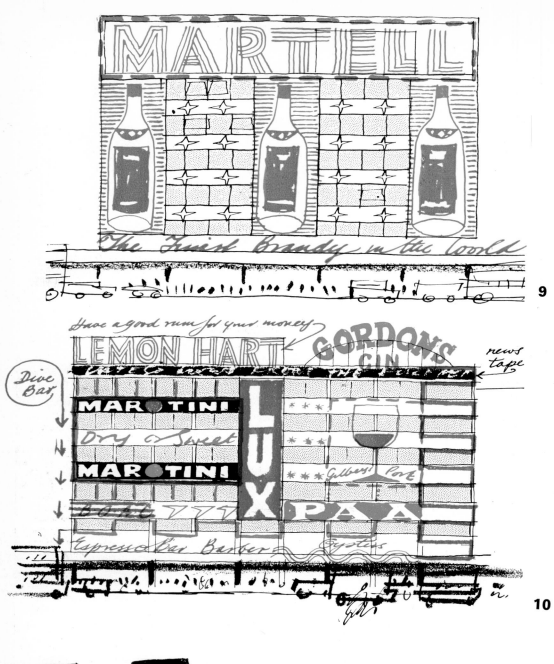

9 MARTELL
The Finest Brandy in the world

10 Have a good rum for your money
LEMON HART GORDON'S GIN
Dive Bar
news tape
MARTINI
Dry Sweet
LUX
MARTINI
Gilbey's Port
BOAC
PAA
Espresso Bar Barber Oysters

11 MARTELL

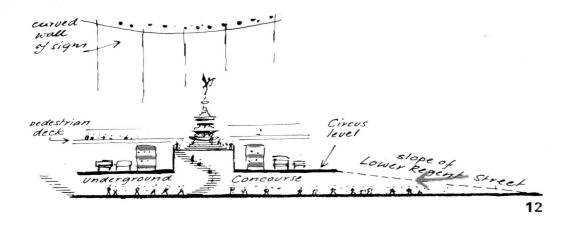

curved
wall
of signs

pedestrian
deck

Circus
level

slope of
Lower Regent Street

underground   Concourse

12

Eros remains a problem. So much part of the Piccadilly Circus we know, his removal would seem unthinkable but the Holford plan showed him still hemmed by railings on a triangular site, thus continuing the present unsatisfactory setting. Why not raise him as 12, with access from the Underground concourse?*

Vital link. From Piccadilly Circus theatreland continues east via Coventry Street, leading into Leicester Square. Look across the circus from Regent Street, and vision ricochets off a series of visual hazards like a pin-table ball – the cascade of stars on the butt end of 'The Prince of Wales' is a case in point. This gambit is important in the entertainment world where customers must not rush through too quickly. The effect is worth keeping if only by projecting signs, 14. If Piccadilly has its deck then this could well continue east to Leicester Square, with an eyeful every inch of the way and with new hotels, restaurants, theatres, etc., leading off the upper deck.

* A further scheme for the Circus area was published in July, 1968. By Dennis Lennon, in conjunction with the Westminster City Council, it was perhaps the most imaginative so far, and also the most realistic in that it represented a massive effort to coordinate site owners and developers. Furthermore it did not treat the Circus in isolation but as part of a larger area, including the whole of Regent Street. (Plans for the latter by Sir Hugh Wilson, acting for the Crown Commissioners, were released at the same time and envisaged the street raised above traffic and covered by a continuous glazed roof.) On the debit side, the scheme for the Circus, with its massive buildings and repetition of square shapes, virtually removed all trace of existing environment, the nostalgic Piccadilly Circus of world-wide affection. Eros became a tiny memento on a vast traffic-free deck while there seemed little visual relationship between this deck and the scene below, with traffic appearing an disappearing in inexplicable directions.

13

Approach to Leicester Square at Upper Level

14

people

traffic

Leicester Square

As it is. This is really the heart of theatreland; also a great opportunity. A place to relax, as its square shape suggests (unlike Piccadilly Circus), with trees, fountains, grass, yet surrounded by all the excitements of showland. The square is a mere shadow of what it was in its Alhambra days, and is now a very half-hearted place. Unable to make up its mind what it should be, it ends up rather a mess.

Good plane trees make a green ceiling over the square but the landscaping underneath is fussy and formless with rustic sheds and a jumble of heavy seating. Worst of all, it is divorced from the sides of the square by traffic, especially on the north side. Fanum House (the AA headquarters) occupies the whole west side and kills it stone dead with its sightless ground floor windows and heavy characterless bulk. By contrast the new Swiss Centre in the north-west corner gives just the sort of uplift needed. Note the alley-way linking through to Charing Cross Road beside the Odeon; though unlovingly done, it gives a sudden welcome from the traffic domination of Charing Cross Road – a view of green trees.

As it could be. First of all traffic should be taken out of the sides of the square, and the whole space reconsidered, while keeping the plane trees. If by some ingenious road-plan Coventry Street could be closed to traffic, then the *Sunday Times* scheme of 1964* would become a starter. This showed both Coventry Street and Leicester Square completely pedestrianized, from the Haymarket turning onwards, colonnaded and lined with trees, Coventry Street forming a quarter-mile long promenade.

If this is not possible then the pedestrian deck might continue from Piccadilly Circus as a covered promenade above the traffic, 14, with steps and ramps down into Leicester Square.

The square itself would be improved by higher buildings around it, topped by plenty of skysigns. Then the perimeter, freed from traffic, should be lined with cafés and bars; their tables spilling out into the square. This would be a welcome place to stop in the whirl of theatreland, a place for bands and open-air exhibitions under the trees, 15. Beyond Leicester Square the pedestrian deck could continue as the spine of theatreland over Charing Cross Road to link up eventually, through a series of squares, to Covent Garden itself. In fact the whole route from Piccadilly to Covent Garden needs rethinking and reviving and any proposals should relate to the problems of the West End as a whole.

* 'In Place of Piccadilly' by Robert Harling, *Sunday Times*, 12th January, 1964.

52

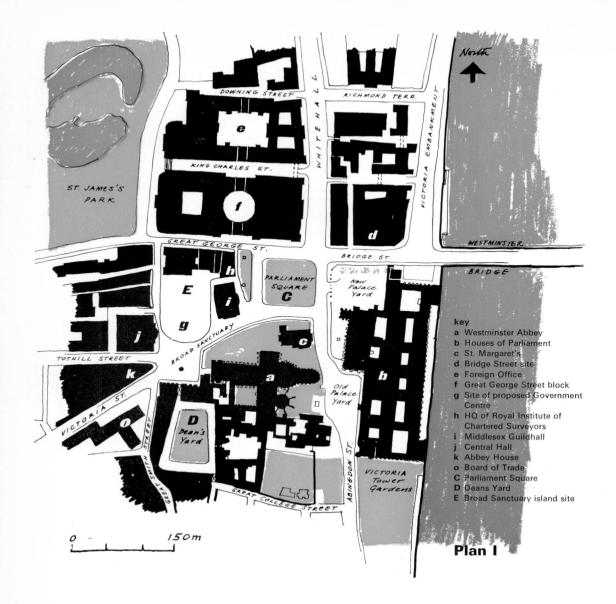

Key labels within the plan:

ST. JAMES'S PARK

DOWNING STREET

RICHMOND TERR.

WHITEHALL

North

VICTORIA EMBANKMENT

KING CHARLES ST.

e

f

GREAT GEORGE ST.

WESTMINSTER

BRIDGE ST.

d

h

PARLIAMENT SQUARE

C

New Palace Yard

BRIDGE

E

i

g

b

TOTHILL STREET

BROAD SANCTUARY

c

a

Old Palace Yard

j

k

o

VICTORIA ST.

GREAT SMITH STREET

D

Dean's Yard

VICTORIA Tower Gardens

ABINGDON ST.

GREAT COLLEGE STREET

0   150m

key
a Westminster Abbey
b Houses of Parliament
c St. Margaret's
d Bridge Street site
e Foreign Office
f Great George Street block
g Site of proposed Government Centre
h HQ of Royal Institute of Chartered Surveyors
i Middlesex Guildhall
j Central Hall
k Abbey House
o Board of Trade
C Parliament Square
D Deans Yard
E Broad Sanctuary island site

Plan I

Civic and Government

The Abbey, Whitehall, the Palace of Westminster and Buckingham Palace are the visible symbols of church and state. The open space formed between the first three, Parliament Square, is the logical setting for pageantry and the natural gathering ground for tourists. Centre of a splendid urban landscape, a national monument in itself, it is also unfortunately one of the six busiest traffic intersections in London, its grass lawned central space made virtually inaccessible by traffic and inhabited only by statues of the famous, 3. The special importance of this place and the need to free it from traffic was recognized in the County of London Plan as long ago as 1943.* This proposed that a considerable area around the Abbey and Parliament should again become a pedestrian precinct, as it virtually was until Victorian traffic engineers shattered it by the Victoria Street–Embankment–Millbank traffic routes. How the resulting Westminster precinct could blossom in townscape terms was later shown by Gordon Cullen in a special issue of the *Architectural Review*.*

* *County of London Plan*. By J. H. Forshaw and Patrick Abercrombie, 1943. Macmillan & Co.

* November 1947: *Westminster Regained*. Later published in book form in *Townscape*, 1961.

Nothing more happened until 1964 when the Government appointed Sir Leslie Martin as its consultant 'to ensure that the various proposals which are under consideration for redevelopment in the Whitehall area are related to each other and have regard to the general architectural character of the area, taking relevant traffic considerations into account.' His brief stated that the Government had decided to rebuild the Foreign Office block and also redevelop the Richmond Terrace–Bridge Street site to provide extra accommodation for Parliament and Government offices. It went on to say that he should also look ahead to the possibility of the eventual redevelopment of other buildings in the area, such as the King Charles Street–Great George Street block of Government offices and the former War Office building. He should also take into consideration building proposals on the Broad Sanctuary island site including the new Government Conference Centre and the rebuilding of the headquarters of the Royal Institute of Chartered Surveyors (see plan I).

In his subsequent report* Sir Leslie Martin stated that in his opinion the building proposals were of sufficient magnitude to create a new setting around, and a new environment within, Parliament Square and that the opportunity should not be lost. He then proceeded to show the form that this new setting might take, backed by a traffic report by Professor Colin Buchanan showing the steps which would be necessary to free the area from through traffic. When published, this report was the subject of considerable controversy particularly in respect of the amount of demolition envisaged. However, there can be no doubt that the Government was right in calling, if belatedly, for a comprehensive plan for this very special place (though as Buchanan pointed out it cannot be dealt with in isolation) and also that the consultant was right in insisting that Parliament Square must be recaptured for people. No system of decking over the traffic should be considered, he said, because of the visual effect on the Abbey and the Palace of Westminster. So far so good, but the sad thing is that his brief seemed to invite a wholesale destruction of existing environment including some very good buildings indeed, notably

* *Whitehall. A plan for the national and government centre.* By Leslie Martin, accompanied by a report on traffic by Colin Buchanan. HMSO, 1965.

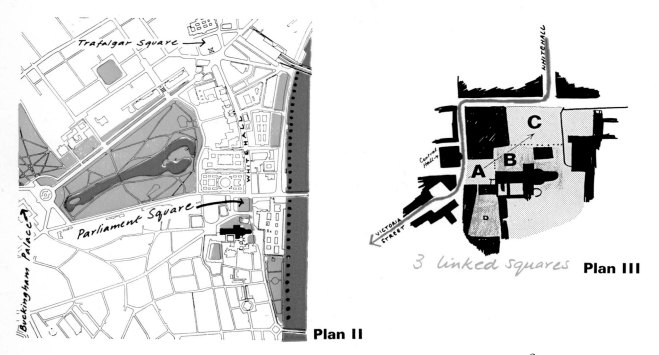

Plan II

3 linked squares **Plan III**

56

the Foreign Office and Gwydyr House. Moreover, the consultant, instead of questioning its validity, appeared to accept it. He then showed how a vastly increased number of civil servants could in fact be housed at the end of Whitehall in a special kind of office building without any increase in height. It was a masterly piece of office planning, but whether it justified the ruthless destruction involved is highly questionable.

As Lord Shawcross said at a public enquiry,* 'there seems to be no administrative advantage and every reason, including administrative convenience, for not concentrating an extra 10,000 civil servants in Whitehall.' For one thing of course it would add considerably to the existing traffic problems, in direct opposition to the Government's declared policy of office decentralization.

* Broad Sanctuary Inquiry, May 1966.

The report gave the impression that it was all or nothing, but was this really true? Surely, what is immediately important, at any rate for the average citizen, is to recapture the space of Parliament Square for public use. Yet, this objective is in danger of being lost in the general controversy, although it could in fact be effected with comparative speed.

4

5

Traffic

4 Approach to Parliament Square from Millbank

5 from Whitehall

Apparently, to quote the consultant's report, 70 per cent of the traffic could be removed:

(a) by the building of an Embankment tunnel road* (shown dotted on plan II). This would have the advantage of not requiring demolition and, as the report points out, makes possible terraces linking Whitehall to the river, today hopelessly separated by a torrent of traffic along the Embankment.

* As first suggested in the *Evening News*, 1956.

(b) by an upgraded east-west route to the south of the area. Horseferry Road was suggested, but Vauxhall Bridge Road may be more practicable, particularly, in view of the future importance of Victoria Station as an inter-continental transport interchange and the inevitable road reorganization involved.* Such action would still leave a much reduced Whitehall/Victoria Street traffic to be dealt with and this might, for the present, follow the line shown on plan III. Such limited traffic along the north side only of Parliament Square need not be harmful to environment provided suitably generous underpasses were provided. In fact it adds movement to the scene. All the rest of the area (shown shaded) could then become pedestrian and at the same time the Parliament extension on the Bridge Street site could go ahead (d on plan I).

* Here the importance of providing a better setting for Westminster Cathedral, shielding it from traffic and perhaps with Ambrosden Avenue paved over and tree-lined, should be explored.

But to get things literally in perspective it is important to study the present townscape at ground level.

6

Whitehall

Link and Curve. The link between Trafalgar Square and Parliament Square is a shallow boomerang curve, and fundamental to the continuity between them is the fact that Whitehall is essentially a street. Looking either way it forms a closure to the view. From Trafalgar Square the curve ensures a changing relationship of the towers and spires of Westminster. It starts off in line with Big Ben, 5, 6, the giant Victoria Tower takes over and finally it ends up pointed at Henry VII's chapel; this gives a leisurely magic which would vanish immediately if Whitehall were straightened out (as suggested in the White- hall report). Coming from Parliament Square, Inigo Jones's Banqueting Hall stands on the angle of the boomerang; key building in a key position. But note that from a distance it is the turrets of the old War Office building next door which do the work and beckon you on. Then, halfway along, as you turn the angle, Nelson's column leaps up emphati- cally to end the vista.

Progression: Whitehall is a progression of imposing buildings, given added scale by contrast with smaller neighbours such as Gwydyr House and those facing the Govern- ment offices at the South end of Whitehall. This give and take suggests democracy far better than any system of rigidly squared up superblocks.* And important to this sense of progression is the punctuation provided by such events as the turrets of the Old War Office seen above already mentioned (clearly seen from the far side of Parliament Square), the impassive Cenotaph and the statues of field marshals, chargers frozen in midstride.

In this built-up curving line, the set-back of the Ministry of Defence was a blunder, somewhat modified by the row of trees in front which continues the line of the street.

From Downing Street a public way could, with advantage, be opened up, penetrating through the Foreign Office and Great George Street blocks via the fine central courtyards,

* Lately, the almost unbelievable arrogance of a Government hellbent on destroying its own historic buildings despite all expert advice, has rallied con- siderable public opposition. An ultimate and ruthless clean sweep of Whitehall seems to be threatened and Government plans made public in December 1969 showed a vast new Home Office building at the Parliament Square end which would necessitate demolition of such important buildings as Norman Shaw's New Scotland Yard and Richmond Terrace one of the last survivals of Georgian domestic Whitehall. At present Crown property is not protected by the planning laws; this must be changed.

58

one square one circular, to Parliament Square. Also, when the Bridge Street site is rebuilt as an extension to Parliament, effort should be made to keep the present striking view up Cannon Row to the Victoria Tower.

Parliament Square

This great open space is largely wasted since access to the centre is virtually denied by the encircling traffic, 3. It is far less used than Trafalgar Square, which is similarly isolated, for there is less incentive (no fountains, lions, or pigeons) and no subways to get there.

Entrances and Exits

Whitehall: seen from Parliament Square there is a fine view up the curve of Whitehall, but the opening is overwide. If Whitehall traffic is reduced, the entrance might be narrowed by projecting the new building on the Bridge Street site out across the line of Whitehall, cutting down the space leakage.

From Westminster Bridge: standing on the bridge, the juxtaposition of the Houses of Parliament and the river is one of the great sights of London. How the suggested tunnel road can be built without destroying the present wonderful feeling of immediacy is a considerable design problem, but if it frees Parliament Square it is probably worthwhile. From the bridge the entry to the square is dominated by Big Ben. Again, a narrowing would be an advantage and the handling of the new Bridge Street building (*d* on plan I), is the key to this. As one approaches, the existing Bridge Street building is on the right and beyond it the Great George Street building which is immensely dignified and should be kept.

From Millbank: the destruction of the terrace in Abingdon Street was regrettable, for in conjunction with the Victoria Tower opposite it held in the space of Old Palace Yard, the entrance to which has now been blasted wide open, 4. This entry, site of the original gateway, should again be restricted.

From Victoria Street: changing direction at Broadway, the ruthless chasm of Victoria Street points at nothing closer than Shell on South Bank. The Abbey gradually emerges, but there is a sawn off, incomplete look about the way the street ends, 8. Gordon Cullen has shown in 'Westminster Revisited'* how a building projected at right angles to the street could be used to lessen its tearaway character and introduce the marvellous and changing drama of verticals waiting there (Abbey towers, St. Margaret's, Big Ben, 1).

From Tothill Street: this narrow high-walled street gives an approach to the Abbey which splendidly emphasizes the verticality of its towers. The west front is approached almost head-on, but the towers only reveal themselves one at a time in a developing view, 2. Finally the Victoria Tower appears also as a surprise visitor.

From St. James's Park (via Great George Street): here the vertical emphasis of the street dramatically frames the giant's pencil of Big Ben, and the turrets of the Great George Street block of Government offices on the left give just the right powerful introduction to the square, right.

* *Architectural Review*, June 1958. Later published in book form in *Townscape*.

Walls

The shape of the square is well defined on the north, south and east sides by large buildings. On the east by the Palace of Westminster, *b*, on the south by the Abbey, *a*, on the north by the Great George Street block, *f*. The latter is exactly right here, strongly holding the side of the square. It has that three-dimensional quality so essential to a corner site like this (see 7), a fine start to Whitehall. Whether it is a good example of this or that style becomes almost irrelevant. As townscape it is fine, a really civic building.

The west wall of the square is different. Here the enclosure is less complete and the buildings, including the Middlesex Guildhall, *i*, are domestic in scale. This is important for, being seen in the same eyeful as the Abbey, they boost the latter's size. Large-scale buildings here would wreck the effect.

Spaces

The present size of Parliament Square seems just right, and the idea of greatly enlarging it (by taking the west wall back to the Central Hall, as the report suggests) would surely be a mistake. It is already as large as Trafalgar Square. Especially without traffic it would then be far too large, and the Hawksmoor towers of the Abbey not powerful enough to stand up to such a large space around them.

But this is more than one big space today, it is in fact part of a series of interrelated spaces around the Abbey (see plan I). For instance, passing between the Guildhall and the Abbey you enter another space, roughly rectangular in shape and dominated by the dome of Central Hall. The great 'captive balloon' of its dome makes an excellent foil to the verticality of the Abbey towers.

The *Victoria Street* approach to *Parliament Square* —

TODAY . . . . AS IT COULD BE

Gulch   8

Gateway   9

Precinct disrupted   10

Precinct regained   11

Suggestions

Traffic now rushes through this space into Victoria Street, but if it were removed (as shown on plans III or IV) there would be the possibility, coming from Victoria Street of angling through three linked squares: the first in front of the Abbey west front, A. The second between the Guildhall, The Abbey and St. Margaret's, B. The third, Parliament Square itself, C (see 11, 11a, 13, 14).

Today, Abbey House (the Victoria Street–Tothill Street corner) strikes into the first space, making you feel as though you were being run down by the *Queen Mary*. When this site is redeveloped the opportunity must be taken of holding in this side of the potential square. Here the slender vertical of the Westminster School memorial excellently pins down the space in front of the Abbey and contrasts beautifully with its soaring towers. (This square is already linked through an arch to the quiet enclosure of Deans Yard with its grass and trees.)

How the removal of traffic and careful use of new building could increase the drama of the Westminster precinct is shown in 9, 11, 11a, 13, 14 and plan IV. For instance, Victoria Street might be stopped visually by a cross building, 9, rather as Gordon Cullen has suggested, but perhaps giving entry to the first square through an arcade of shops. At the same time it would provide an interestingly shaped pedestrian space at the end of Victoria Street with an alternative approach to the square giving the slit view seen in 1. The Central Hall (powerful but coarse in detail) is probably best kept as a 'captive balloon' and partly masked by a new building on the Broad Sanctuary site, *m*, brought forward to the original site boundary to form a small square (A) in front of the west end of the Abbey (still about 60 m. square).* This would give a splendid launching pad for the towers from a restricted space, the sort of immediacy impossible to obtain from the spaces shown in the Whitehall plan.

There could be cafes and shops for tourists and visitors, at ground level on the Broad Sanctuary site (thus avoiding the depressing effect of looking into offices, at ground level, as in the new development around St. Paul's, for instance). A hollow centre to the building might form an enclosed court of small shops, while the roof could provide a splendid viewing platform. Below ground would be extensive multilevel parking for visitors' cars and buses with exit on foot direct into the new Broad Sanctuary Square, A.* The landscaping of the three potential squares requires a special study in itself, but the aim would be to define them by the floor surface, belts of trees and change of level.

SQUARE A

* In the competition for the new building, won by William Whitfield, the rules insisted that it should be set back to expose the Central Hall.

* The use of part of this site for a Government conference centre was confirmed as a result of Sir Robert Matthew's report (March 1967) on the Broad Sanctuary Inquiry. He recommended that provision should also be made for tourists and visitors.

Plan IV. *Parliament Square a could be. Arrowed numbers indicate viewpoints of drawings. (Key as for Plan II but in addition m, Government conference centre over shops at ground level; n, shopping arcade. Dotted line shows alternative route for limited traffic.)*

← Middlesex Guildhall

Parliament Square

St Margaret's

12

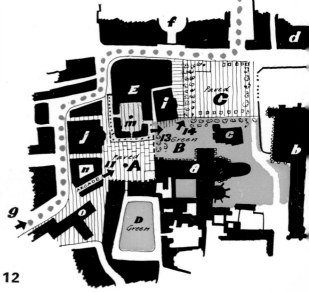

...fés & shops at ground level in new building on Broad Sanctuary site

Middlesex Guildhall

i

a

c

b

Kenneth Browne

SQUARE B (grass & trees)

Middlesex Guildhall

Great George Street block retained

new parliamentary offices

i

f

d

b

SQUARE C — *Parliament Square*

*Pimlico Gardens
looking towards
St. George's Square*

Lillington estate

1a

64

2

Pimlico

The street pattern of Pimlico is so confusing that you almost need a compass to get for instance to Victoria Station from the river at Grosvenor Bridge. You find yourself tacking through a series of angled grids which seem determined to take you off course. Added to this there is no Underground. As plan 1, p. 66 shows, Pimlico is contained by a rough triangle, Victoria Station at the apex and the river forming a curving base. The east side is Vauxhall Bridge Road; the west the railway lines from Victoria. In between lies a bewildering maze of streets which results from the grid parallel to Vauxhall Bridge Road, Belgrave Road and St. George's Drive being suddenly cut through by Lupus Street and changing direction by 45 degrees (to strike the river more or less at right angles). Add Warwick Way which slices across at random between Ebury Bridge and Rochester Row, and direction is soon lost. Here you rely on landmarks – the church towers, the trees in the squares and recently the tower block in Stag Place. The latter orientates you immediately at the otherwise hopeless six-way junction where Denbigh Street crosses Belgrave Road, and ends the view up Denbigh Street with authority.

Pimlico is a mainly residential district and probably best kept that way. Comparatively inexpensive, by contrast with its grander neighbour Belgravia, it has a lively shopping area including a street market around the junction of Warwick Way and Tachbrook Street (M on plan 1).

Places

The main features of Pimlico are its nineteenth-century squares, Eccleston (A on plan), Warwick (B), and St. George's (C), together with the huge red 1930's bulk of Dolphin Square (F), and Churchill Gardens (E), the extensive Westminster council estate by Powell and Moya. The typical Pimlico landscape however still consists of 1850 stucco terraces, mostly fag-end classical but still with much that is worth retaining. The long curving riverfront is a potential asset here which is almost entirely neglected, save at the south end of St. George's Square where it becomes Pimlico Gardens, 1, 2. Along the embankment, Grosvenor Road carries heavy traffic and thus effectively cuts off the housing from the river. Though there is a splendid view across to Battersea Power Station from Churchill Gardens (the smoke from the power station is another matter and urgently needs attention) in general the Nine Elms bank opposite is just a scruffy mess badly in need of imaginative redevelopment. It is the site of the future Covent Garden market which must be designed in such a way as to enhance the river views.

The luxury flats of Dolphin Square and the various Westminster council estates, notably Churchill Gardens and the new estate in Lillington Street (by Darbourne and Dark*), account for a considerable part of the total area of Pimlico. It is interesting to compare them with each other and also with the nineteenth-century squares. Taking the squares first, both Eccleston (1835) and Warwick (1843) look like Belgravia, Thomas Cubitt having been the developer of both districts. Lying at right-angles to Belgrave Road, which continues the spine of Belgravia into Pimlico, the squares are grand in scale with five-storey terraces round a central treed space approximately 213 m long by 92 m across. In neither is the classical detail particularly good, Eccleston being the better of the two, but a grandeur of scale and unity is achieved through sheer size, rhythm of projecting porticoes and unifying cream-painted stucco. The latter shows up the magnificent plane trees in the central gardens to perfection.

Warwick Square is given added interest by a church spire at its west end (see 8).

St. George's Square (C on map) is by contrast very elongated (approximately 335 m long) stopped at the north end by St. George's Church and at the south end open to

*Highly successful outcome of a public competition.

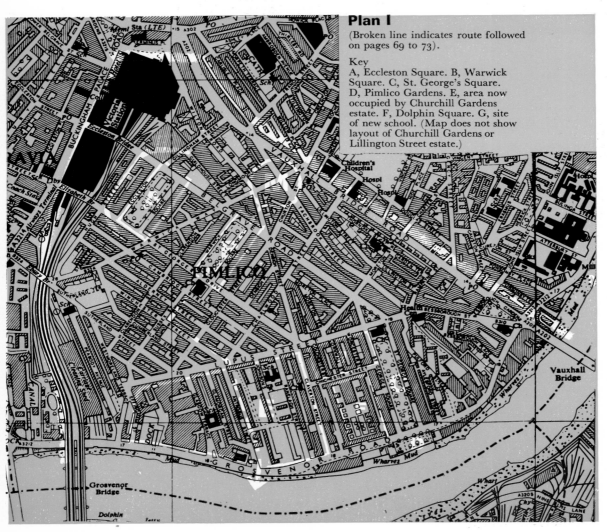

Plan I
(Broken line indicates route followed on pages 69 to 73).

Key
A, Eccleston Square. B, Warwick Square. C, St. George's Square. D, Pimlico Gardens. E, area now occupied by Churchill Gardens estate. F, Dolphin Square. G, site of new school. (Map does not show layout of Churchill Gardens or Lillington Street estate.)

3

the river. Again, regular terraces to either side and a tree-filled central space give a satisfying unity, reinforced by the repetition of balconies and porticoes. Along the west side of the square is a distant view to the tower of Westminster Cathedral, 1. Unfortunately the south end is separated from the river by the heavy traffic along Grosvenor Road, though the space is continued on the other side of the road by Pimlico Gardens. The latter, a riverside garden, is the one place on the mile of river between Vauxhall and Grosvenor bridges which really uses the waterfront as public amenity.

Churchill Gardens, E: Good modern architecture, well landscaped and particularly striking when seen from the Grosvenor railway bridge. From there the trim repetition of parallel slab blocks at right angles to the river reminds one of berthed liners, an impression reinforced by the nautical roof line. Yet from inside it does not give that feeling of place which the older squares have. This may result from the staggered height of the various blocks, four, eight, nine, ten storeys which, coupled with perspective, have the effect of disrupting the enclosure. The environment is very good indeed when carefully photographed but often worryingly broken up when you walk through it. Existing buildings have been incorporated into the scheme, some successfully, as for instance All Saints Church, some only working from one viewpoint like the Balmoral Castle pub, 3, which from certain angles looks like a left-over hunk of cheese. The gardens and planting are particularly well handled throughout.

Dolphin Square, F. This is the other extreme. Where at Churchill Gardens space tends to fall out, it is here rigidly, even oppressively, contained by the regular ten-storey wall of building which encloses the central green space. However, the surrounding wall is a good sound barrier to the traffic outside and given better architectural expression the 'private world' idea has its merits.

Areas to Keep

In planning the future of Pimlico, and deciding what to keep, Eccleston, Warwick and St. George's Squares must take priority. It is important, too, that their immediate surroundings should be carefully considered and the protection of Eccleston Square (like Westminster Cathedral), when Victoria is rebuilt as a large continental interchange station, needs careful study. Massive road works are bound to be entailed and a careful survey is needed now to decide which streets should be retained and which can go, for they vary very much in quality. Some are important on account of position, for instance the Cambridge Street terrace which forms the background to St. Gabriel's Church when looking from Warwick Square. Some, such as Clarendon Street behind Eccleston Square and Churton Place, 6, should be kept on merit, while others might be rebuilt keeping the basic street pattern. What should not happen in urban design terms is unfortunately demonstrated on the north-west side of St. George's Square. Here a large site, g, between Chichester and Lupus Streets, was recently cleared for a new GLC secondary school. No matter how good the new building may be, there has been a ruthless disregard for the effect on St. George's Square. The regular wall of buildings enclosing the square has been broken to allow what must be a disastrous leakage of space.

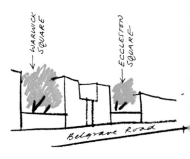

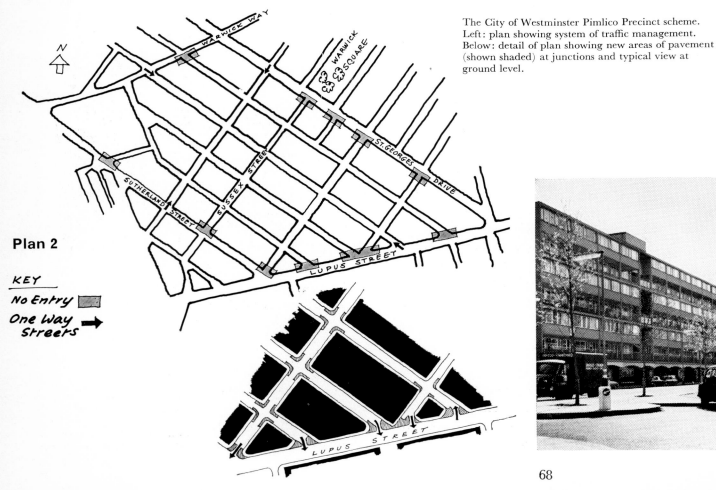

The City of Westminster Pimlico Precinct scheme. Left: plan showing system of traffic management. Below: detail of plan showing new areas of pavement (shown shaded) at junctions and typical view at ground level.

Plan 2

KEY

No Entry

One Way Streets

Traffic

The whole of Pimlico is harassed by traffic, much of it taking short cuts across the residential streets. It is particularly heavy in Belgrave Road where its noise intrudes on Eccleston and Warwick Squares and some form of wall (left), at the end of each square would be worth considering to act as a barrier. Again, as we have seen, Grosvenor Road along the embankment is almost impossible to cross so that there is the exasperating situation of an unusually long stretch of river front housing which is divorced from the water by the traffic. Between Churchill Gardens and the river for instance there is just a vast stretch of tarmac, while Bessborough Gardens by Vauxhall Bridge is an extreme example of space made unusable by circulating vehicles.

In an attempt to defeat the short cut takers, the Westminster council have carried out an experimental traffic management scheme in the residential grid between Sutherland Street and St. George's Drive. Plan 2 shows how entrances to the area were limited to one on each side and the road ends narrowed down by paving with tree planting at the street corners.

from the market area 5

LINKING

via Churton Place 6

under Belgrave Road 7

Linking

This kind of action could surely be just the beginning of a series of limited schemes aimed at making conditions better for pedestrians while at the same time forging links in what is at present so confusing an area. For instance Sussex Street,* which centrally crosses the grid shown opposite, could become entirely pedestrian except where it is intersected by

* This is already a street of some interest with shops and pubs. Though in places it could be improved by rebuilding it is particularly attractive at the south end, where it meets Lupus Street.

into Warwick Square **8**

— then down Sussex Street (reclaimed from traffic) **9**

TODAY **9a**

10

Vacant Site

TODAY

some rebuilding keeping existing scale — turn left down Winchester St.

Churchill Gardens

—then under Lupus Street (traffic masked by single storey shops) **11**

13

.. into Churchill Gardens .. along footpath ..

streets. The stretches between streets are short (only three or four houses), so the inconvenience of occupier/drivers would be minimal, while the environmental gain could be great. This, combined with such measures as for instance turning the existing vacant plot shown in 10a into a small park, 10, could become the backbone of a pedestrian route joining the market area around Warwick Way and Tachbrook Street (via Warwick Square, Sussex Street and Churchill Gardens) to the river (see broken line on plan 1). An idea of how this might look in practice is shown in sketches and photographs 5 to 16, culminating in a riverside terrace opposite Battersea Power Station, reached by a deck over Grosvenor Road.

TODAY **14a**

The Balmoral Castle →

Up ramp to deck over existing garages and bridging Grosvenor Road ·**14**

. . and out on to riverside promenade raised above the traffic **15**

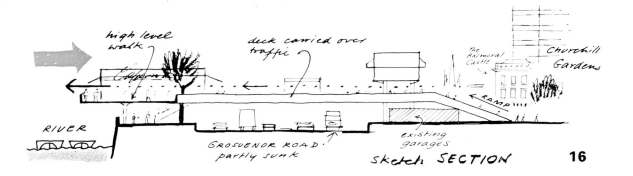

high level walk

deck carried over traffic

The Balmoral Castle

Churchill Gardens

RAMP

RIVER

GROSVENOR ROAD partly sunk

existing garages

sketch SECTION

16

Riverside

Today this is a mess and entirely wasted except for Pimlico Gardens, p. 74. Single storey warehouses, a GPO workshop, a garage and a petrol station block views of the river. Failing a sunken riverside highway here when terraces could link across the traffic to the river, what can be done? Sketches below and over the page show some of the possibilities. Save for gimmicky shelters and over-prominent seats, Pimlico Gardens is very pleasant as it stands – just a river wall, a statue, well-kept grass and two rows of fine plane trees. Indeed it should hardly be touched and certainly not gingered up. Most important, too, it is not an endless draughty stretch of park. It is small, even snug, a place to sit and watch the river, bounded at either end by high walls over one of which cranes appear. Any alterations to it should not destroy what exists but follow the idea in a series of linked spaces – for instance (as shown below and over) starting from Vauxhall Bridge, the high arched walls of the single-storey warehouses might be kept and a river walk run over the top. Then Pimlico Gardens, entered through an archway in the existing wall, needs little change, as we have seen; even the greenhouse should be kept. However, the connection to St. George's Square across Grosvenor Road remains a problem. The road might be bridged as shown in the sketch (in which case it should

AS IT COULD BE —

existing trees →

Grosvenor Road

promenade

river

a promenade over warehouses with — steps down to playground

*then through an archway
into the quiet of
Pimlico Gardens
(walled garden)*

replace poorly designed
shelters – keep greenhouse

PIMLICO GARDENS

existing wall defines
boundary of garden

ramp up to
deck over
road

wall acts
as baffle to
traffic noise

*∴ then along river wall
past existing wharf*

74

steps up to restaurant garden

...and under a new riverside restaurant overhanging the water — at the far end steps lead up to the promenade opposite Churchill Gardens

take the form of the square being carried over the road, not just a flimsy bridge) or effected by an underpass. Between Pimlico Gardens and Grosvenor Bridge the route would follow the river, first past an existing but refurbished wharf, then under a new riverside restaurant (with private garden) and eventually connecting with the deck in front of Churchill Gardens seen in 15.

1   2   3

Mayfair

The word Mayfair suggests elegance, leisure, *pâté de foie gras*, gracious eighteenth-century squares. But times have changed and the swing from aristocratic residence to business use has modified the picture; the private house has been replaced by the flat and the glossy advertising agency; day-life has speeded up, night-life slowed down.

But despite the change of use and much rebuilding,* Mayfair still retains a distinctive flavour; it still demonstrates certain principles of civilized urban life, while at the same time, money and prestige ensure that its buildings are kept in first-class repair. Fortunately the GLC and Westminster City Council seem intent on holding the present character as far as they can, on resisting rebuilding and even on encouraging a return to residential occupation.

* Especially in the twenties when many of the great private houses were ruthlessly torn down, some to make way for giant hotels named after them.

Shape

Though Mayfair is based on a gridiron plan, this does not become worrying for several reasons. Firstly, because of the interesting townscape which occurs when two gridirons intersect at an angle, as in the Berkeley Square area. This results in strange places like the charming little garden tucked away behind the Grosvenor Chapel in South Audley Street. Secondly, because of the variety provided by a wealth of pedestrian streets. Notable are Shepherd Market where the original May Fair was held, and the arcades

4

leading from Piccadilly, the latter spick and span, dead straight and gleaming like well-oiled rifle barrels. Piccadilly Arcade in particular, 4, is splendid with its gleaming ripple of full height bow windows.

But mainly the grid works because, while giving an appropriate sense of order, it is relieved by the squares and the proximity to the royal parks. These squares, the great English contribution to urban living, are essentially domestic rather than grand manner, designed as terraces of private houses standing round a central green space, the houses forming the neutral frame to a well-treed communal garden. Though today all too many of the surrounding buildings in Mayfair squares have been replaced (unlike Bedford Square, Bloomsbury, which retains its original appearance), the central oasis of forest size trees nearly always holds the environment together and goes far to mask discrepancies in

5

scale and detail. For instance Berkeley Square, 5, is still fine despite the fact that both the east and south side are now occupied by ponderous and undistinguished buildings. In summer at any rate the mass of foliage is still the dominant factor. In the gridiron of streets there are in fact few places where you are out of sight of the trees of at least one square.

Threats to Squares

What happens when the earlier thick planting is disturbed is only too sadly demonstrated in Grosvenor Square. Here the original William Kent landscaping was replaced, as a setting for the Roosevelt memorial, by a dreary layout of rigid paths and axial planting. Over sixty fine mature trees were felled in the process of turning it from a 'square' into a 'municipal garden'. This mistake should be rectified and great care taken that it is not repeated elsewhere. But coupled with the danger of unsympathetic replanting is the constant pressure to build car-parks under squares. Here is space free of buildings, the argument runs, so it is the obvious place; furthermore, the work can be done with little disturbance to present appearance. But this is quite certainly untrue. Plausible, tempting, but one of those short-term traffic expedients which must be resisted for the sake of environment. The effect of interfering with the drainage of large trees is unforeseeable and the chance of such trees surviving slight. And in the case of Berkeley Square, which has the most beautiful tree-cover of any square in London, it would be impossible to put a car-park underneath without destroying a large percentage of the trees, and hence the whole magnificent effect. For an awful warning look at Cadogan Place. Rebuilding around squares also needs the most careful control, especially regarding height.

Access to Parks

An attractive feature of Mayfair has always been its proximity to the royal parks, giving a welcome contrast of tightly built up environment and the illusion of countryside (even to sheep in Hyde Park). This immediacy has been eroded by the ever-increasing traffic along the dividing lines, culminating in the massive widening of the Park Lane Improvement Scheme. This, despite careful landscape treatment, remains a piece of ruthless and ill-judged traffic engineering, and forms a great barrier between Mayfair and Hyde Park, 3. Undoubtedly this road, or part of it, should have been sunk to preserve the link between the two. Indeed, the whole practice of slicing off the edges of the royal parks for road widening must be deplored. *

Erosion. Mayfair is a good example of an environmental area which is subjected to an unacceptable level of traffic, much of it bound elsewhere and taking a series of zigzag short cuts. In addition, one-way traffic systems have turned squares into race circuits, cutting off the buildings from the central space and making the crossing of shopping streets, notably Bond Street, almost impossible.

Scale Threatened. Satisfactory contrasts in scale between house and mews flat or between say Albany Chambers, 2, and the Royal Academy next door, has in many cases been wrecked, the most ruthless example being the brutal insertion of the Hilton Hotel which makes its neighbours in Park Lane look like dolls' houses. In fact Park Lane has been ruined by unsuitable building while from the north side of Mayfair, Oxford Street threatens to encroach with massive faceless slabs.

* The south side of Hyde Park is also threatened in this way.

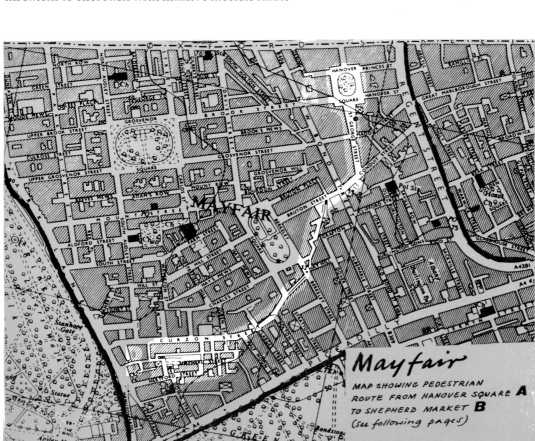

Mayfair

MAP SHOWING PEDESTRIAN ROUTE FROM HANOVER SQUARE **A** TO SHEPHERD MARKET **B** (see following pages)

Hanover Square as it could be (View South) **6**

Action

It is most important that the present character should be kept and reinforced. This means a check on rebuilding, and draining extraneous traffic from the area, particularly from the squares. If these cannot become entirely pedestrian, then their central space might be linked on at least one side to the surrounding buildings as 6. Somehow the present trend for traffic to take over all available ground space must be reversed so that inside Mayfair walking routes can be re-established. This need not mean closing down whole streets but choosing those places which best lend themselves to pedestrianization. This will have to be determined by careful townscape survey and will entail such measure as blocking the ends of streets and turning some small streets into arcades. *

If we apply this sort of thinking to actual places we might take the short section of Bond Street where it widens out at the junction with Burlington Gardens. A small pedestrian square here would seem natural and conveniently connect with the Burlington Arcade and the Albany.

* Here the new Economist building in St. James's Street (by Peter and Alison Smithson) should be mentioned as a rare instance where pedestrian space has been gained by the imaginative provision by the architects, of a small pedestrian square raised up from the surrounding streets.

View S. down St George St now. **7**

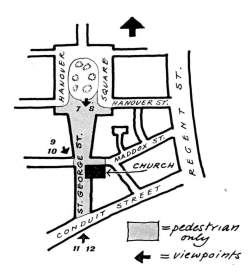

Plan showing St. George Street pedestrianized

8   **9**

As it is · · ST. GEORGE STREET Looking South · · As it could be

Example: Linking. To give an instance of a pedestrian route, some of which already exists, while the rest is in embryo, we might take the route (followed in 7–16) which angles across from Hanover Square to Shepherd Market. The former today affords perhaps the worst example of a central space divorced from its buildings by the traffic. But standing near the Chantrey statue of William Pitt, the view south down the funnel of St. George Street is, despite some unsympathetic buildings, still potentially one of the best in London, with the portico of St. George Street, Hanover Square, projecting out into the roadway, 7.

This Italianate vista is now seen across a torrent of traffic from nearby Regent Street while St. George Street itself is almost solid with parked cars. But if the traffic could be taken out of the south side of the square and St. George Street, this could become a fine start for a series of linked pedestrian spaces, 6, with the trees of the square carried on to soften the rather bad corner buildings. Even if the whole street cannot be pedestrianized then the south or narrower end seen in 8, 9, including the church certainly should be. This tapering street is excellent townscape and just right in scale for the pedestrian. The eastern half of the upper stretch and a short length of Maddox Street beside the church should also be paved. Here note the fine three-quarter view of the church from Regent Street. Conduit Street would still carry traffic but the view back from it up St. George Street, which is now traffic filled, 10, would look like 11. From Bruton Street the walk might continue down Bruton Lane by the Coach and Horses, 12. Narrow and zigzagging, this lane is today a gap-toothed mess. But it could look like 13.

10   **11**

As it is . . ST. GEORGE STREET FROM CONDUIT ST. . . *As it could be*

At the end of it we come out at the bottom of Hay Hill which falls steeply down from Dover Street. Here it would be possible to deck over the junction with Berkeley Street in a

12   **13**

As it is . . . . . BRUTON LANE *. . . . . As it could be*

14

16

15

SHEPHERD MARKET

rebuilding of the north side of Hay Hill; a deck reached on the level from Dover Street and linking over the traffic to the south end of Berkeley Square.

Cross Berkeley Street into Lansdowne Row – an existing pedestrian street with small shops on either side. Single storeyed, they seem rather mean and give an insufficient feeling of compression. However they provide a welcome refuge from cars just the same. At the far end, where the row joins Curzon Street there was, until recently, a flight of steps, a familiar and precious piece of pedestrian articulation between differing levels. This has gone, presumably sacrificed to gain road-width – a typical example of the way the rights of the city walker are whittled away to ease the traffic. Further on along Curzon Street the footpath suddenly angles left and tunnels through an archway into Shepherd Market. Immediately the mad rush of the traffic outside gives place to a quiet world of small-scale buildings, a little square and a criss-cross of pedestrian alleyways, 14 to 16. The pressure is off, you can go slow, shop from a barrow, 15, eat out on the pavement, watch other people. In fact you are in the kind of intimate, human scale environment which must be included in any future development of Mayfair and which here must be safeguarded at all costs. *

* The pedestrian route might then continue south from here under Piccadilly to Green Park.

1

Bloomsbury

The story of Bloomsbury is a sad one. Perhaps London's finest example of a planned and civilized environment, it is nevertheless in grave danger of obliteration.

To make things worse, the main threat comes, not from the speculator, which would be bad enough, but from two of our leading cultural institutions, London University and the British Museum (see page 92).

Character

Since the squares, 1, terraces 2, and alleyways 3, of Bloomsbury form a hierarchy of spaces, the balance between them is vitally important. Human in scale and essentially English, Bloomsbury displays no grand gestures, but an easy relationship between things and a gentle development from one real place to another.

Pattern

Though the area is built to a grid, it shows that, given ingenuity, much variety can still be achieved. Though long vistas such as Gower Street and Southampton Row become a bore, the space between them has considerable variety. Also the east-west streets never seem to run straight through.

Following the prototype squares, Covent Garden (1630) and Lincoln's Inn Fields (1658) Bloomsbury Square (1660) was the first open space to be so called. Laid out by the Earl of Southampton to face his mansion, it was a fortunate start for the subsequent development of Bloomsbury. To quote Sir John Summerson, the Earl 'realized that a square was not enough by itself. It had to be the centre of a number of smaller, less

84

2

expensive streets, and perhaps a church. In fact the whole thing had to have a life of its own'.* Bloomsbury was organic from the start.

* *Georgian London* by Sir John Summerson, Penguin Books 1962.

After Bedford Square (1776), 1, the pattern was developed north and east, principally by James Burton and Thomas Cubitt in a splendid series of squares: Russell, Torrington, Woburn, 4, Gordon and Tavistock. Throughout, the principle of Georgian town planning, the creation of urban units catering for all classes, was reflected in the variety of scale yet homogeneity of the whole. The buildings by Thomas Cubitt for the Bedford Estate between Russell and Euston Squares, notably Gordon Square and Tavistock Square, were particularly well designed and soundly built. So much so that, to quote Summerson again, 'their execution (is) so admirable that today there is hardly a wall out of straight or a sagging lintel.'

In contrast to the squares, Cubitt also built a small shopping centre (now Woburn Walk, 3) of small stuccoed houses with shops on the ground floor. Exceptionally refined in detail and human in scale they are a model for today and must be safeguarded.

3

4

5

Squares

The squares of Bloomsbury are unlike the Continental baroque squares, which were only elements in a grand composition. Here are no axes or grand vistas, but instead each square forms a small world of its own, casually linked by undemonstrative terraces to other such worlds. The squares differ widely in size and shape, but always contain a central garden of large forest trees, left unpruned as though in a rural landscape. The regimented facades of the houses contrast happily with informal and luxuriant foliage. Built to be quiet and calm, away from the traffic of the main streets, the enclosure afforded by the surrounding buildings of equal height gives much the same effect as being in a room. Non-directional, it suggests contemplation rather than movement.

6
7

8

Lincoln's Inn

9

A band of simple iron railings always enclosed the central garden, effecting a neat junction between its informality and the formality of the architecture, but only in Bedford Square have these survived the wartime drive for scrap. Elsewhere they have been replaced by scruffy concrete posts and pig-wire. It is essential for the appearance of the squares that either railings similar to the original should be replaced, or, in some cases, that there should be no vertical barrier at all.

Wanted: a survey

Here of all places it is the spaces and connections which count, the preservation of single buildings is not enough. The importance as urban landscape is such that here again a detailed townscape survey is urgently needed to determine what must be kept at all cost and what action is needed to pull back areas which have slipped down. This survey would cover not only the famous places, such as the splendid green oasis of Gray's Inn, 6, 7, an object lesson to planners, a world of quiet courtyards and tree-shaded lawns within a few yards of the traffic, or Bedford Square, 5, the last square to remain intact, where only protection is needed. But the survey would also cover the lesser known places like Regent Square, 15, rundown and war-damaged, where imaginative action is desperately needed, and draw attention to the value of strange places like St. George's Gardens, 9, just south

New Square Lincoln's Inn

10

of Regent Square, a secret garden hidden from the racket of the streets and immensely valuable in human terms. And south again the three adjacent spaces – Brunswick Square – Coram's Fields – Mecklenburgh Square, a symmetrical composition which, since the removal of the Foundling Hospital which stood in the middle, makes no kind of townscape sense, while Coram's Fields itself an untidy dustbowl. Here again ideas are needed. In particular attention needs to be drawn to the area south and east of Queen Square as far as Gray's Inn Road. Threatened with redevelopment, it contains a number of fine streets, notably Great James Street, 12, Rugby Street, Great Ormond Street (south side); and in Doughty Street – John Street – Bedford Row, a complete Georgian street scene. These must not be broken down by piecemeal redevelopment. Queen Square itself is a sad mess, badly in need of improvement, the forbidding hospital buildings which occupy the whole east side literally put the hand of death on the whole place. The south side remains attractive.

Threats

Traffic: stationary cars packed into every available space detract visually from the squares, 13, but any suggestion to put car parks under them must be discounted. Without doubt it would kill the trees which account for at least half of Bloomsbury's attraction. More serious still, since noise and exhaust fumes are added to visual disruption, is the introduction of one-way traffic systems which have brought fast-moving traffic where it has no right to be. Gower Street for instance has become a race-track, sending vehicles tearing across the east end of Bedford Square. This must be stopped and Bloomsbury recognized as an environmental area with all through traffic excluded.

Guildford Street

11

12

traffic 13

church now
demolished →

gap
↓

neglect 15

unsuitable building 14

Unsuitable building: in addition to the deadly boredom of most of the London University buildings, the council flats, 14, 16, in the north-east corner of the area, behind St. Pancras Town Hall, are a prime example of how not to build in Bloomsbury. A depressing failure in environmental terms they lose all sense of urbanity by spilling out anonymous chunks of open space on to the pavement in grisly contrast to the earlier Bloomsbury with its respect for space and enclosure. If this is the twentieth century pattern, it is just not good enough.

16

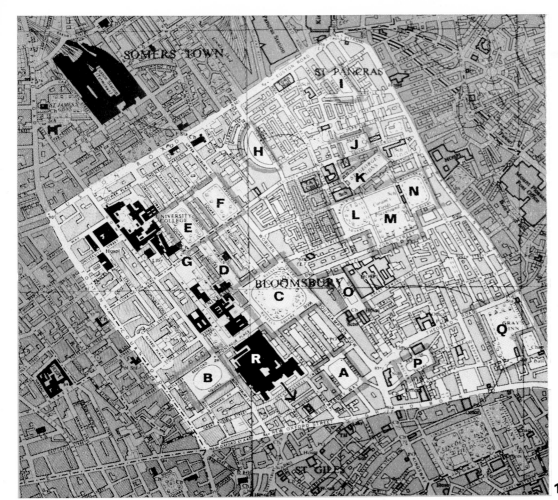

17

Commercial pressures: the monstrous office blocks of Theobolds Road and Holborn threaten to spread into Bloomsbury itself. This tendency must be arrested, for they would smash the scale to pieces.

Neglect: Regent Square, 15, is a prime example of neglect. A tree-planted square with a Georgian church at one end, complete with portico and steeple (St. Peter's by William Inwood, 1824). Something worth keeping, you would think, despite the fact that the body

18

of the church was blitzed. Yet, instead of carefully rehabilitating the place, we find that not only do the council flats which now occupy the north side leave gaping holes at the corners of the square, but the church itself has now been demolished. Apparently the Church Commissioners regarded it as an embarrassment and its scenic importance was not recognized by the Camden Council.

Expansion: this is the greatest threat of all. For a long time the British Museum has wanted more space, and it planned to develop a 7-acre site* immediately south of the existing building. This necessitated demolishing the whole west side of Bloomsbury Square and erasing Great Russell Street, 19, and all the small streets between it and Bloomsbury Way. Fortunately objections by the borough of Camden have now been upheld by the Government and the scheme has been dropped. In addition to supplying the required museum accommodation, including a National Library, this scheme also provided a raised pedestrian piazza as large as Bloomsbury Square between the church and the Museum. But unless this piazza had been brilliantly handled, it would have been just another draughty desert nobody wanted, while London would have lost another well-loved area of character. Though few of the buildings involved are outstanding in a pedantic sense, the spaces they enclose and the atmosphere they create are valuable, 23. What is more, the Museum itself, 20, would be unlikely to gain visually from being further exposed, especially as seen from a raised deck. The present powerful railings, reinforced by the avenue of trees in Great Russell Street, help the rather dull design. In addition to this Hawksmoor's St. George's Church gains by its present siting embedded in the street line in the same way as many Italian churches. This is not to defend the existing buildings to either side but the way they make you see the church – first the portico casually encountered in the line of shops along Bloomsbury Way, 24; then the tower, surprising enough anyway and doubly so by the way you are made to see it, 21. Another experience here is the way you have to squeeze round the base of the church to get to the church hall and Little Russell Street, forced to be literally in touch with the material and detail of the building, 22. Such subtleties are important as townscape yet all the time they are being whittled away.

* Bounded by Great Russell Street, Bloomsbury Street, Bloomsbury Way and Bloomsbury Square.

19

20

21 23

22 24

However the real tragedy of Bloomsbury is the presence of London University. Grown out of all recognition since its arrival as University College in Gower Street in 1825, it has in the last thirty years acted like some monstrous cuckoo. Ever greedy for more space, it now threatens the very existence of this area which on the face of it appears to provide such a suitable and historic background. Squares have been smothered and valuable environment sacrificed to make way for student hostels and halls, mainly bulky, dull buildings, overpowering in scale, and contributing nothing. Outstandingly bad is the hideous Faculty of Engineering block facing Malet Street. Surely it is time to call a halt and insist that further university growth must take place outside Bloomsbury.

A plan published in 1959* demonstrated how the considerable further expansion envisaged by the University might fit into the existing pattern of Bloomsbury. It showed a series of enclosed and tree-filled spaces, bounded by long horizontal terraces and with a tower block in Endsleigh Street. Terraces would complete the enclosure of Russell Square, a much needed step, and also bridge over the present entrance to Woburn Square which would become pedestrian. This plan had the merit of being comprehensive and unifying in intent; it proposed buildings whose layout would contain open spaces which people could enjoy, something the previous buildings, save for the original building in

* By Sir Leslie Martin and Trevor Dannatt.

Gower Street, had signally failed to do. Unhappily the plan appeared also to involve considerable demolition of existing and precious things – for instance the Cubitt terrace on the east side of Gordon Square, and the whole of Woburn Square as it now stands including the church, 4, 29. The square would even lose its present form entirely with a long block running slap across the middle. This threat to Woburn Square, which few people probably realized, became more imminent with the concrete proposals for the area north of the existing university senate house in 1967. This scheme, unaccountably passed by the Royal Fine Art Commission, creates a pedestrian precinct between Russell Square and Gordon Square which is fine, but then not only demolishes the terrace and church seen in 4 and 29 (replacing them by stepped back wings to a terrace in Bedford Way), but also smashes the present plan of the square (see plan below). This cannot be justified, for no matter how good the new architecture may be, it destroys a valuable piece of the original Bloomsbury pattern. Also, in detail, the visual effect of a stepped back block (replacing an even-height terrace) seen in profile on the north side of Russell Square, will surely be disruptive.*

* Since this article was written belated efforts to save Woburn Square have failed. Appeals to the Minister of Housing and Local Government, Mr. Greenwood, received the reply that he had decided 'not to intervene at this late stage' – a deplorable decision.

Despite efforts, too little and too late, to arrest this sad example of wilful destruction, demolition has begun and the terrace seen in foreground of 29 is already a pile of rubble.

Interlocking old and new

Woburn Square today is a long rectangle with the church built flush with the east side terrace, 4, 29. Down the centre of the square a mass of huge trees masks the damage already done to the west side with the insertion of the Warburg Institute. The square's value in spatial terms is that it forms an excellent link between the king-sized Russell Square and the smaller Gordon Square to the north. With traffic removed it would be even better.

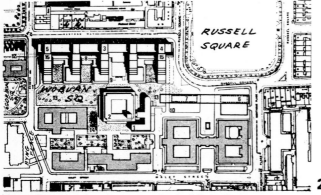

Above: Plan showing the proposed rebuilding of Woburn Square by London University which will completely wipe out the present character of this square. 26-29, the present approach from Russell Square to Woburn Square showing, 26, the gap which exists on the west side of the former.

29

Surely then it would be possible to keep the existing form of the square, yet still put a new university terrace down the gap-toothed west side of Bedford Way as proposed. This would follow the precedent of the British Museum which does not destroy one side of Bedford Square but lies behind an existing terrace. If this were done the transition from Russell Square could be as shown in 30 to 33, with the enclosure of Russell Square completed, Woburn Square cleared of traffic and, at the north end, leading into a re-modelled Byng Place (G on map, no.17). This with traffic rerouted might become a central paved university square, 35, with car park underneath and dominated by the existing University church of Christ the King. It could connect to the green spaces of Gordon and Woburn Squares through entrances restricted by rows of bookshops, cafes, etc., and with a series of smaller quadrangles running south from it. Today all this is either harrassed by traffic or scattered with parked cars.

Internal street

An imaginative scheme* which, unlike those for London University, does not threaten outstanding environment, is that for part of the Foundling Estate, the area bounded by Bernard Street, Marchmont Street, Tavistock Place and Hunter Street (see shaded area on map). A combined operation between a developer and the council, it promises a remarkable structure consisting of a large sandwich of shops at ground level with two levels of car parking underneath. The shops will be reached from a broad internal and traffic-free street, open for much of its length save for covered sidewalks and a large central glazed shopping hall. The flat roof of the shops will form a continuous plateau,

* By Patrick Hodgkinson (consulting architect for Estate, Sir Leslie Martin).

95

Line of existing terrace continued by new University block – completing enclosure of Russell Square

a

g

30

another new building bridges entrance to Woburn Square

g

c

h

Woburn Square freed from traffic and entered . . . .

31

e

. . through a colonnade under the new building h

32

Approach to Woburn Square .. *AS IT COULD BE*

four acres in extent, enlivened, it is hoped, with pubs, cafés, trees, etc. and bounded on either side by long raked-back terraces of housing for Camden Council. The success of the scheme will depend largely on the handling of the big central space. Can it

BYNG PLACE *TODAY*

Pavd Square
(with car park under)

BYNG PLACE as it could be

become a real place in the way the old squares are or will it be just another great draughty open deck? Protected on both sides by the terraces, it promises to avoid the wind-swept aridity of Route 11 but the scale looks ominously large. This redevelopment will provide a new west side to Brunswick Square and the opportunity to improve it as townscape. The intention is to omit the housing directly opposite the square so that the central space of the new scheme and the square itself can be directly related. A pedestrian bridge between the two will link them further. Today, as we have seen, the adjoining spaces of Brunswick Square – Coram Fields – Mecklenburgh Square make little visual sense. Here is the chance to unify and improve them and also to link them with their surroundings.

Kenneth
Browne

Green
Square

UNI

University Square

Key
a, Southwark Bridge
b, Blackfriars Bridge
c, Waterloo Bridge
d, Hungerford Bridge
e, Westminster Bridge
f, Waterloo Station
g, Shell tower

South Bank New Town

Why new town? Because here, on South Bank, is the golden opportunity to build a new West End to relieve the pressures on the old. Before the existing West End is completely wrecked, development pressures should be diverted here, to an area absurdly undeveloped considering its central position. Where also, unlike the present West End, there are few good buildings which must be kept. However, unless the chance is seized now it will be frittered away in unco-ordinated rebuilding.

The argument that the area is too remote is seen to be invalid when you look at the map (see facing page). The area of South Bank which directly affects the West End, that is between Lambeth and Blackfriars bridges, is contained in a great curve of the river with St. George's Circus equidistant from the City, Fleet Street and Westminster and the Festival Hall no further from the Strand than Piccadilly Circus. Again the shortest route between Westminster and the City is via South Bank. Distance is no

NEW TOWN

objection, but precedent and communications are. Worth noting however is the fact that the removal of Shell to South Bank has already stimulated commercial interest there and this is likely to grow.

As for communication, the important thing is visible connection. The area must be linked to the present West End in such a way that the river ceases to be thought of as a barrier. Also there needs to be a strong enough magnet to attract the crowds as the Festival of Britain did in 1951.

If the opportunity is wasted, it will be for lack of sufficiently bold conception of what it might become. Piecemeal rebuilding will then obstruct future opportunities and high building, not directed to any overall effect, wreck it as urban landscape. Another danger

Promenade in front of Royal Festival Hall

is an over-emphasis on culture. Zoned as a 'cultural centre' by the GLC, the riverside could easily become too stodgy, a perch for culture vultures only.

Character

This would be a pity, as for centuries South Bank was London's pleasure ground and could be so again. The success of the Festival of Britain showed that. Then, for a brief season, the whole place was set alight, with bands, gay crowds and light-hearted buildings brilliantly set against the changing backdrop of the river. This set the pace, giving high hopes for the future of South Bank: hopes so far unrealized.

As long ago as 1949 Gordon Cullen foresaw the danger* that strict zoning might turn this into 'a cultural centre enveloped nightly in gloom' if the vitality injected by the forthcoming Festival was not maintained. Again, in 1951,* he showed how this could be avoided, using the ideas thrown up by the Festival but in a more permanent form. Today these lessons seem to have been forgotten. It is time we relearnt them.

* 'Bankside Regained' by Gordon Cullen. *Architectural Review*, January, 1949. Also in *Townscape*.
* 'South Bank Translated' by Gordon Cullen. *Architectural Review*, August 1951. Also in *Townscape*.

The main object must be to bring the South bank within the orbit of the West End. Sky-signs should advertise its attractions across the river; it should contain theatres, dance halls, exhibitions, restaurants, bowling alleys, pubs, sports arenas, pleasure gardens, bandstands, the lot, reached from the river itself by gay landing stages and waterside piers. Also there should be plenty of houses for people who want a cosmopolitan life near the centre of London.

Scale

However, only if it is tackled in a big way can this be made to work, so formidable are the traffic problems. Indeed, it seems clear that this is a case for rebuilding on a multilevel system, with complete segregation of people above traffic, not the half-hearted measures no one bothers to use. With few buildings which must be preserved, unlike the present West End, here is the chance to do things on a sufficiently large scale (learning from the draughty mistakes of Route 11).

Waterloo station seems to be the key. At the centre of the river's curve, its platforms are already at a raised level and even now, you can walk above the traffic from the station to the opposite side of the river. (And to see how cleanly this can be done, look at the bridge spanning between buildings across York Road). It is easy enough, then, to imagine Waterloo redeveloped as a giant transport interchange, possibly combined with a new Charing Cross station. The latter moved south of the river, with travelator links to the

Strand, as Professor Buchanan has suggested. The new combined station would have concourses, squares and a network of pedestrian spaces lined with shops at the present platform level (i.e. above the traffic) and rising from them high towers of offices and flats. In fact, office buildings, rightly discouraged elsewhere in central London, could well be encouraged here where secondary transport would be unnecessary.

River Views

The river must be the starting point in considering the South Bank as townscape, for here are the most important views in London, views which in some cases have already been

sadly marred by the mad folly of allowing high buildings near St. Paul's. This has reduced the splendid dome in some cases (as seen from Hungerford Bridge, above) to merely one incident among many. Enough to make Canaletto weep.

But if, for instance, you look across to South Bank from Victoria Embankment in front of the Temple you see a stretch of riverside which cries out for attention. To the right, is the new site of the National Theatre, previously just a sad mess of unrelated stores, warehouses and sheds with the ungainly bulk of the Shell building rearing up on the right like some giant's wardrobe. The whole scene is as inspiring as cold porridge, yet here is a magnificent site right opposite Somerset House, one of the finest buildings in London.

At present it is as scruffy as Tilbury; this stretch of river could look very different with a concentration of new building such as we have described; perhaps becoming a shallow pyramid of towers, the highest over Waterloo station and along Waterloo Road and with multi-level lower buildings terracing down to the Thames. The foreshore should be alive with entertainments of all kinds closely linked to the river with its jetties and pleasure

craft. This concentration of high towers at Waterloo in the centre of the river bend would also work visually from all angles up and down stream and not obstruct the remaining views of St. Paul's, (see drawing below). Also the now disruptive vertical of Shell above would be neutralized, absorbed in the general massing 1.

1

Live Link

But the effectiveness of any attempt to revive the South Bank will depend largely on the closeness with which it can be linked to the West End. The links must seem inevitable and inviting. Hungerford bridge, the present foot route to the Festival Hall, is today as dismal as it could be – a bleak catwalk on the side of a railway bridge, so narrow that two people can scarcely pass. But this bridge is in an important strategic position, for it points straight at the heart of the West End, at Leicester Square and Piccadilly Circus.

The present structure, an eyesore anyway, should be replaced in such a way as to offer a direct pedestrian link between the Strand, South Bank riverside and Waterloo station. Broad and lined with shops, cafés and pubs, it should be a street crossing the water, 6, and with a restaurant in the middle giving splendid views up and down river, 2. It could be glazed against the weather and its form would depend on the transport needs (A and B show in diagram two versions, with and without the railway). If Charing Cross station were moved to South Bank, then a travelator system would be incorporated in the bridge for rapid cross-river transit, with wide footpaths for more leisurely walkers. Such a broad high-level connection, would help to break the seemingly impassable barrier created by the Shell complex But the bridge structure must not be so bulky as to obstruct the important river views to Parliament and St. Paul's.

South Bank Riverside

Here then is the chance to give London a real waterfront, something missing for the last 200 years. But, south of Westminster Bridge the scheme for rebuilding St. Thomas's

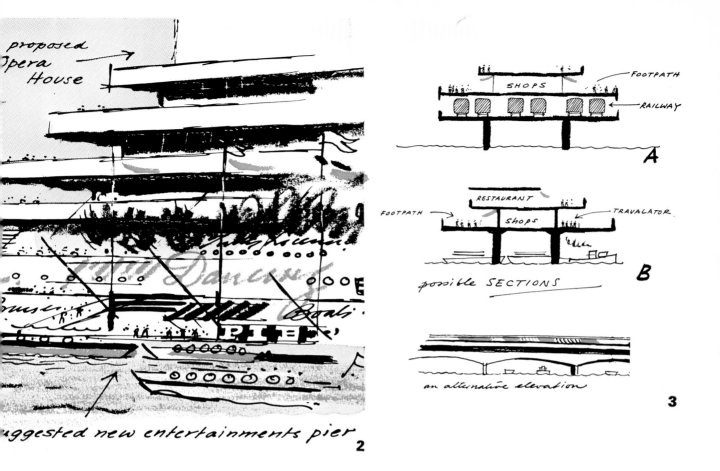

proposed Opera House

suggested new entertainments pier

2

FOOTPATH
SHOPS
RAILWAY

A

FOOTPATH
RESTAURANT
shops
TRAVALATOR

possible SECTIONS

B

an alternative elevation

3

Hospital looks extremely unsuitable. The existing buildings have a fine skyline and present a quiet and civilized frontage of repetitive court and wing to the river. They are good cross-river neighbours to the Houses of Parliament, deferring to the importance of the latter. But the design for the new hospital suggests an attempt to cram too much on to a limited site and in consequence the sheer bulk of the proposed building right on the riverside is likely to overpower the Palace of Westminster opposite.

North of Westminster Bridge, the stretch which most concerns us here, the danger is that having rightly kept the roads away from the river, unlike on the Victoria Embankment opposite, and so made a traffic free river walk possible, the GLC will end up by making it all too polite; just chunks of building standing well back from an over-wide promenade. This has happened already between Westminster and Waterloo bridges and it looks as though the same treatment may be intended right up to Blackfriars. This must not happen. Today, when you come down from Westminster Bridge, the draughty promenade in front of County Hall is like bureaucracy personified – no joy anywhere. It doesn't matter if the joy comes later, as it did in 1951 when the great space next door, vacant ever since, was filled with people and gay lights. Today it is just a respectable over-wide promenade. This was the former site of the National Theatre and Opera House and Denys Lasdun's design for them suggested a brilliant solution to a difficult problem. Faced with building directly in front of Shell, what do you do? Wisely, instead of trying to compete with the great, soulless office cliffs and tower, he used them as a foil to his multi-terraced composition, which had a strong but lively facade to the river (see page 108). Since the riverfront itself needs more interest than the present

4

the riverside walk should pass under buildings.

Royal Festival Hall

Dancing BOAT

Live Lin Shopping

5

featureless wall, this might be provided by a large entertainment pier and boat station running through beneath Hungerford Bridge and along it in front of the Festival Hall. Placed directly opposite Charing Cross, the magnet needs to be at full charge.

Under Hungerford Bridge you come out in front of the Royal Festival Hall complex. Impressive buildings are well linked by terraces on massive columns and the ramps and steps are bold and imaginative. But still the promenade runs, wide as a race track, in front of them and by now you begin to feel the strain – especially in our climate.

In 1951 this was the site of six cantilevered lookout platforms (designed by Eric Brown and Peter Chamberlain for the Festival). These sailed gaily out over the river: light elegant structures in contrast with the permanent buildings behind, they gave just the right, carefree note that was needed and now needs to be recaptured. But th guardians of 'culture' won and the platforms have gone.

Sense of River

But it is this sense of river, a feeling of intimate contact with boats, watermen and gulls, which people want, and those lookout platforms were one way of expressing it. Apart from piers and jetties there are many other ways in which the necessary immediacy can be captured. Sketches 5, 7, 8 show three. One way is to bring buildings out over the

river so that the walk passes underneath them. From above you have the sensation of being afloat, while below there is shelter (glazed or open) – enclosure replaces exposure. (Remember the 1951 Riverside Restaurant.) Elsewhere pedestrian squares might be raised over the traffic and bounded by terrace houses overlooking the river, with slot views down to it; a slice of river brought into the town, 8. The river walk could continue by the waterside but steps would lead up to the contrasting enclosure of the squares.

Again, the river could be indented to form small protected harbours, dramatized by the immediate juxtaposition of large buildings. Dredging would be necessary or some form of boom to retain the water at low tide, but the effect could be splendid, 7 (as at Queenhithe Dock east of Blackfriars Bridge, the nearest thing to Venice in London).* The river walk is shown passing through the colonnade of a theatre with steps down to the water. By such means the Thames would be possessed by the riverside walker instead of remaining remote and tamed beyond a sheer, monotonous wall.

* The City of London, ever ready to sacrifice its best townscape, is in the process of destroying all this.

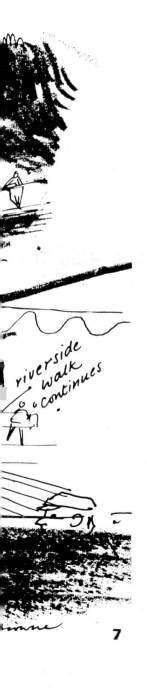

riverside walk continues

7

riverside walk

slot view of river from pedestrian square
raised over traffic.

8